# English G 21

## Freiarbeitsmaterialien 1
## Klasse 5
## Kopiervorlagen

Cornelsen

**English G 21**

# Freiarbeitsmaterialien 1
# Klasse 5
# Kopiervorlagen

*Im Auftrag des Verlages herausgegeben von*
Prof. Hellmut Schwarz, Mannheim

*Erarbeitet von*
Silvia Gilbert, Düsseldorf
sowie Helmut Dengler, Limbach

*In Zusammenarbeit mit der Englischredaktion*
Dr. Christiane Kallenbach (Projektleitung);
Olivia Gruver (verantwortliche Redakteurin);
Bonnie Glaenzer (beratende Mitwirkung)

*Illustration*
Eva Muszynski, Berlin

*Umschlaggestaltung und Layoutkonzept*
Klein & Halm Grafikdesign, Berlin

*Layout und technische Umsetzung*
Eva Miller-Matthia, MatMil Translations & Desktop Publishing, Berlin

*Titelbild Hintergrundfoto*
IFA-Bilderteam, Ottobrunn
(Union Jack: Jon Arnold Images)

**www.cornelsen.de**
**www.EnglishG.de**

1. Auflage, 3. Druck 2010



Druck: H. Heenemann, Berlin

ISBN 978-3-06-031922-0

Inhalt gedruckt auf säurefreiem Papier aus nachhaltiger Forstwirtschaft.

# Vorwort

## Autonomie im Unterricht

Die vorliegenden Materialien zur Freiarbeit bieten den Schülern vielfältiges Material zur spielerischen Überprüfung gelernter Inhalte an. Dies ist für die Schüler gerade im Hinblick auf die weithin geforderte Lernerautonomie von großer Bedeutung.
Freiarbeit bedeutet vor allem selbstbestimmtes Arbeiten. Die Schüler werden dabei schrittweise dazu befähigt, Verantwortung für das eigene Lernen zu übernehmen. Sie haben hier die Möglichkeit, das eigene Lerntempo zu bestimmen.
Alle Materialien können von den Schülern anhand des Lösungsschlüssels am Ende des Heftes selbst überprüft werden, sodass der Lehrkraft an dieser Stelle des Unterrichts mehr die Rolle des Lernberaters zukommt. Die Lehrkraft kann sich dadurch vor allem den schwächeren Schülern zuwenden und unterstützend tätig werden. Auch sollte die Lehrkraft darauf achten, dass sich die Schüler bei Partner- und Gruppenarbeit in der Zielsprache austauschen und die angegebenen Redewendungen benutzen.

## Spielerischer Lernprozess

Die vorliegenden Freiarbeitsmaterialien bieten oft spielerische Ansätze und sollen die Schüler dazu motivieren, sich mit der Zielsprache zu beschäftigen. Die Sammlung enthält neben Spielen auch Partnerarbeitsmaterialien, um das gemeinsame Lernen zu fördern. Wenn die Klassensituation dies ergibt, können bei Partnerübungen z.B. ein schwächerer und ein stärkerer Schüler zusammenarbeiten, wobei der stärkere dem schwächeren Schüler Hilfestellung bietet und dadurch auch sein eigenes Wissen festigt.

## Binnendifferenzierung

Gerade in Klassen mit einem breiten Leistungsspektrum bieten sich die Freiarbeitsmaterialien auch für den Einsatz bei der Binnendifferenzierung an. So werden schwächere Schüler individuell gefördert und stärkere Schüler gefordert.

## Zielgruppe

Die Freiarbeitsmaterialien sind für alle Ausgaben von English G 21, Band 1, konzipiert und unitweise aufgebaut. Die Materialien können sowohl einzeln als auch in Partnerarbeit bearbeitet werden. Langfristig wird so die soziale Kompetenz gefördert. Es ist von entscheidender Bedeutung, dass sich die Schüler gegenseitig helfen und korrigieren.

## Benutzung der Materialien

In den Übersichtsseiten vor den Units wird der jeweilige Schwerpunkt der einzelnen Arbeitsblätter kenntlich gemacht. Dieser kann auf Grammatik, Redemitteln oder Wortschatz liegen. Dadurch können die Materialien sowohl im normalen Unterricht zur Vertiefung eines Schwerpunkts oder zur Wiederholung eingesetzt werden, ebenso wie in ausgewiesenen Freiarbeitsstunden.
Dort, wo etwas ausgeschnitten werden muss, wurde dies durch das Symbol der Schere kenntlich gemacht. Es bietet sich an, die Materialien zu folieren, um sie haltbar zu machen.

# Inhalt

## Unit-Überblick

Unit 1 – Überblick .......... 8
Unit 2 – Überblick .......... 16
Unit 3 – Überblick .......... 24
Unit 4 – Überblick .......... 33
Unit 5 – Überblick .......... 41
Unit 6 – Überblick .......... 50
Lösungen .......... 59–64

## Kopiervorlagen

| | Nummer | Titel | Schwerpunkt |
|---|---|---|---|
| **Welcome** | 0.1 | Welcome! | Kennenlernspiele zur Aktivierung der Vorkenntnisse aus der Grundschule. |
| **Unit 1** | 1.1 | Ship ahoy: Schiffe versenken | Übung zur Versprachlichung der Uhrzeiten. |
| | 1.2 | How we say and write dates | Schreibübung zum Ausschreiben von Daten. |
| | 1.3 | Dominos | Grammatikübung zum Singular und Plural von Substantiven. |
| | 1.4 | Make your own sentences | Übung zur selbstständigen Bildung von Sätzen. |
| | 1.5 | Calendar word search | Wortschatzübung zum Thema *days* and *months.* |
| | 1.6 | Colours cryptogram | Wortschatzübung zum Thema *colours.* |
| | 1.7 | Go fish! | Übung zur Versprachlichung *have got* anhand eines Kartenspiels. |
| **Unit 2** | 2.1 | Match the verbs | Grammatikübung zum *simple present.* |
| | 2.2 | Michael's school day | Schreibübung zum Ausschreiben der Uhrzeiten. |
| | 2.3 | Family cryptogram | Übung zu Verwandtschaftsverhältnissen. |
| | 2.4 | Scrambled family words | Wortschatzübung zum Thema *family.* |
| | 2.5 | Maggie's family tree | Übung zum Leseverstehen. |
| | 2.6 | Pet shop ads | Schreibübung zum thema *pets.* |
| | 2.7 | Home sweet home | Wortschatzübung zum Thema *house* und *furniture.* |

| | Nummer | Titel | Schwerpunkt |
|---|---|---|---|
| **Unit 3** | 3.1 | Sports quiz | Schreibübung zum Thema *sports* und *hobbies.* |
| | 3.2 | Laura's bedroom | Wortschatzübung zum Thema *clothes.* |
| | 3.3 | Opposites | Bastelspiel zu Gegensatzpaaren. |
| | 3.4 | Shopping | Übung zum Leseverstehen zum Thema *shopping.* |
| | 3.5 | Pounds and pence, euros and cents | Übung zur Verschriftlichung/ Versprachlichung von Preisangaben. |
| | 3.6 | Michael's week | Schreibübung zu Häufigkeitsadverbien. |
| | 3.7 | Maggie visits her grandparents | Lückentextübung zu Fragewörtern. |
| **Unit 4** | 4.1 | Birthday invitation | Wortschatzübung zum Thema *party.* |
| | 4.2 | At Sarah's party | Grammatikübung zum *present progressive.* |
| | 4.3 | A bottle of ... | Lückentextübung zum Thema Lebensmittel und Behältnisse. |
| | 4.4 | My body | Wortschatzübung zum thema *body.* |
| | 4.5 | *Some* or *any*? | Schreibübung zu *some* und *any.* |
| | 4.6 | Personal pronouns | Grammatikübung zu Personalpronomen. |
| | 4.7 | Funny food | Schreibübung zum Thema *food.* |
| **Unit 5** | 5.1 | Did you ...? | Grammatikübung zum *simple past.* |
| | 5.2 | When I was your age ... | Übung zum Leseverstehen in Verbindung mit dem *simple past.* |
| | 5.3 | What did Michael do yesterday? | Schreibübung der Uhrzeiten in Verbindung mit dem *simple past.* |
| | 5.4 | Match the verbs | Grammatikübung zum *simple past.* |
| | 5.5 | Tangrams | Bastelspiel zum *simple past.* |
| | 5.6 | Letter mix | Grammatikübung zum *simple present, present progressive* und *simple past.* |
| | 5.7 | Morris the tennis star | Schreibübung zu *how many* und *how much.* |
| **Unit 6** | 6.1 | What are you doing? | Schreibübung zur Satzbildung. |
| | 6.2 | Word partners | Grammatikübung zu Kollokationen. |
| | 6.3 | I usually ... | Grammatikübung zum Unterschied zwischen *simple present* und *present progressive.* |
| | 6.4 | Jane's chores | Grammatikübung zum *present progressive.* |
| | 6.5 | *This/these* or *that/those* | Lückentextübung zu *this/these* und *that/those.* |
| | 6.6 | Group words | Schreibübung zur Festigung von Vokabeln und Oberbegriffen. |
| | 6.7 | You have to ... | Grammatikübung zu Präpositionen. |

Start

1

Go to 8
2

3

What's your name?
4

Go to 25
21

22

Where are your mum and dad from?
23

24

What's your favourite colour?
25

26

Go back to 23
27

28

What's your telephone number?
29

30

What's your favourite number?
31

32

Go back to 29
33

34

What are the days of the week?
35

Finish!

Where do you live?
20

19

Have you got a pet?
18

17

Go back to 14
16

15

- Play the game in groups of four.
- You will need a dice and four counters.
- If you answer a question right, roll again.
- If you answer a question wrong, it's the next student's turn.

**********************

- Dieses Spiel ist für vier Schüler.
- Man braucht einen Würfel und vier Spielsteine.
- Wenn du eine Frage richtig beantwortest, darfst du noch mal würfeln.
- Wenn du eine Frage falsch beantwortest, ist der nächste dran.

What's the time?
14

13

Do you like bananas?
12

11

Go back to 4
10

9

Have you got a brother or a sister?
8

7

How old are you?
6

5

# Unit 1 – Überblick

## KV 1.1 Ship ahoy: Schiffe versenken

Partnerarbeit: Dieses Spiel übt das Versprachlichen der Uhrzeiten. Falls die S das Spiel nicht kennen, sollte L die folgenden Regeln kurz erläutern oder auf Folie bereitstellen.
Jeder der Spieler zeichnet fünf Schiffe waagerecht und/oder senkrecht in der ersten Tabelle ein, ohne dass der Partner sie sieht, und zwar:

- zwei Schiffe, die aus zwei Feldern bestehen;
- ein Schiff, das aus drei Feldern besteht;
- ein Schiff, das aus vier Feldern besteht;
- und ein Schiff, das aus fünf Feldern besteht.

In der zweiten Tabelle kann jeder Spieler die Treffer oder Fehltreffer eintragen, die er beim Partner gelandet hat.
Ziel des Spiels ist es, herauszufinden, wo die Schiffe des Partners sind, indem man einen Tag und eine Uhrzeit nennt, z.B. *Tuesday at quarter past seven*. Wenn dort nichts ist, antwortet der Partner *Missed*. Wurde ein Teil eines Schiffes getroffen, ist die Antwort *Hit*. Ist das ganze Schiff erwischt, sagt man *Sunk*. Gewonnen hat, wer zuerst alle Schiffe des Partners „versenkt“ hat.

## KV 1.2 How we say and write dates

Eine Übung, die den Unterschied zwischen Schreibung und Aussprache von Daten thematisiert. Die Ergebnisse werden in Partnerarbeit verglichen.

## KV 1.3 Dominos

Nachdem die S die Dominosteine ausgeschnitten haben, sollen die Substantive im Singular mit ihrem Plural verbunden werden. Eine Steigerung des Schwierigkeitsgrades ist dadurch möglich, dass die S eigenständig die richtigen Singularformen nennen, bevor sie die entsprechenden Dominosteine suchen.

## KV 1.4 Make your own sentences

In dieser Übung haben die S die Möglichkeit, eigene Sätze zu bilden, indem sie die einzelnen Wörter mit farbigen Linien verbinden und dann die Sätze entsprechend aufschreiben. Soll ein Wort in unterschiedlichen Satzverbindungen verwendet werden, können neue Kombinationen durch die Verwendung unterschiedlicher Farben gekennzeichnet werden. Man kann aber auch die einzelnen Wörter ausschneiden lassen, sodass die S die Wörter zu jeweils einem neuen Satz zusammenlegen und dann aufschreiben können.

## KV 1.5 Calendar word search

Die S können auf spielerische Art und Weise die Namen der Wochentage und Monate wiederholen und festigen.

## KV 1.6 Colours cryptogram

Diese Aufgabe übt die englischen Farbwörter. Ein Kryptogramm ist ein Geheimcode, bei dem bestimmte Nummern bestimmten Buchstaben zugeordnet sind. Die S können durch die ersten vier Gleichungen den Code knacken und anschließend die geheime Frage lesen.

## KV 1.7 Go fish!

Dieses Kartenspiel ist angelehnt an die Quartettspielerfahrungen der S. Alles, was man braucht, ist ein normales Kartenspiel ohne Joker. Die S üben durch das Spiel Fragebildung und Kurzantworten der wichtigen Verbform “have got”.

My name: ______________________________

| | | | | | | | |
|---|---|---|---|---|---|---|---|
| Monday | | | | | | | |
| Tuesday | | | | | | | |
| Wednesday | | | | | | | |
| Thursday | | | | | | | |
| Friday | | | | | | | |
| Saturday | | | | | | | |
| Sunday | | | | | | | |

My partner's name: ______________________________

| | | | | | | | |
|---|---|---|---|---|---|---|---|
| Monday | | | | | | | |
| Tuesday | | | | | | | |
| Wednesday | | | | | | | |
| Thursday | | | | | | | |
| Friday | | | | | | | |
| Saturday | | | | | | | |
| Sunday | | | | | | | |

# KV How we say and write dates

*Complete the sentences. Check your sentences with your partner.*

*Vervollständige die Sätze. Vergleiche deine Sätze mit denen deines Partners.*

**Marc: 25/11/1977**

We write: *Marc's birthday is on 25th November.* ____________

We say: *Marc's birthday is on the twenty-fifth of November.* ____________

____________________________________

**Janice: 23/7/2004**

We write: ____________________________________

We say: ____________________________________

____________________________________

**Valentine's Day: 14/2**

We write: ____________________________________

We say: ____________________________________

____________________________________

**Christmas Day: 25/12**

We write: ____________________________________

We say: ____________________________________

____________________________________

**Your birthday?**

We write: ____________________________________

We say: ____________________________________

____________________________________

*Cut out the boxes and match the singular noun with its plural noun.*

*Schneide die Boxen aus und verbinde die Substantive im Singular mit ihrem Plural.*

| | |
|---|---|
| **Start!** | exercises |
| plate | pencils |
| school | **Finish!** |
| box | teachers |
| ruler | babies |
| exercise | shops |
| pencil | friends |

| | |
|---|---|
| family | kites |
| shop | dogs |
| friend | families |
| teacher | plates |
| baby | schools |
| kite | rulers |
| dog | boxes |

# KV Make your own sentences

*Use the words to make your own sentences and write down as many as you can.*

*Benutze die Wörter, um eigene Sätze zu bilden. Schreib so viele Sätze wie möglich.*

*I have got an English friend.*
*This is the new student.*

book

school

an

can

old

the

I

am

go

have got

friend

nice

ten

like

English

a

we

is

are

teacher

years

at

new

this

student

*Find these 19 words:*

*Finde diese 19 Wörter:*

~~MONDAY~~
~~TUESDAY~~
WEDNESDAY
THURSDAY
FRIDAY
SATURDAY
SUNDAY
JANUARY
FEBRUARY
MARCH
APRIL
MAY
JUNE
JULY
AUGUST
SEPTEMBER
OCTOBER
NOVEMBER
DECEMBER

| | | | | | | | | | | | | | | |
|---|---|---|---|---|---|---|---|---|---|---|---|---|---|---|
| A | S | K | T | N | U | J | V | F | B | D | X | C | Z | D |
| O | B | M | J | A | N | U | A | R | Y | E | B | M | F | P |
| C | R | W | C | C | E | L | W | I | X | C | L | A | L | E |
| T | U | E | S | D | A | Y | Y | D | I | E | O | P | Y | O |
| O | Q | D | Z | X | F | Z | N | A | W | M | A | R | C | H |
| B | I | N | J | T | G | M | A | Y | H | B | K | I | D | N |
| E | P | E | L | H | Q | O | Y | W | V | E | T | L | X | F |
| R | H | S | E | P | T | E | M | B | E | R | V | Z | N | M |
| A | O | D | S | I | H | Y | O | Z | U | U | A | S | O | G |
| G | F | A | M | R | U | P | N | A | G | B | Q | C | V | R |
| B | N | Y | U | J | R | V | D | H | T | J | J | L | E | H |
| D | O | M | L | K | S | X | A | U | G | U | S | T | M | P |
| S | A | T | U | R | D | A | Y | L | S | N | J | D | B | I |
| C | E | P | N | Q | A | W | I | R | K | E | E | J | E | R |
| S | U | N | D | A | Y | Q | F | E | B | R | U | A | R | Y |

**Sunday** ____________________

____________________

____________________

**Monday** ____________________

____________________

____________________

**Tuesday** ____________________

____________________

____________________

**Wednesday** ____________________

____________________

____________________

**Thursday** ____________________

____________________

____________________

**Friday** ____________________

____________________

____________________

**Saturday** ____________________

____________________

*Match the letters and the numbers to find out the colours and the secret question.*

*Ordne die Zahlen den Buchstaben zu, um die Farben und die geheime Frage herauszufinden.*

| A | B | C | D | E | F | G | H | I | J | K | L | M | N | O | P | Q | R | S | T | U | V | W | X | Y | Z |
|---|---|---|---|---|---|---|---|---|---|---|---|---|---|---|---|---|---|---|---|---|---|---|---|---|---|
| | 14 | 16 | | 12 | X | | 21 | 22 | X | 26 | | 10 | 13 | | | X | | 7 | 25 | | X | 5 | X | | X |

| | | | | | | | | | | | | | | | | |
|---|---|---|---|---|---|---|---|---|---|---|---|---|---|---|---|---|
| Y | | | | O | | + | | | U | | = | | | | | |
| 17 | 12 | 6 | 6 | 4 | 5 | | 14 | 6 | 15 | 12 | | 3 | 1 | 12 | 12 | 13 |

| | | | | | | | | | | | | | |
|---|---|---|---|---|---|---|---|---|---|---|---|---|---|
| | | | | | + | | | D | = | | | | |
| 5 | 21 | 22 | 25 | 12 | | 1 | 12 | 2 | | 8 | 22 | 13 | 26 |

| | | | | | | | | | | | | | | | | |
|---|---|---|---|---|---|---|---|---|---|---|---|---|---|---|---|---|
| | | D | + | Y | | | | O | | = | O | | | | | |
| 1 | 12 | 2 | | 17 | 12 | 6 | 6 | 4 | 5 | | 4 | 1 | 18 | 13 | 3 | 12 |

| | | | | | | | | | | | | | | | |
|---|---|---|---|---|---|---|---|---|---|---|---|---|---|---|---|
| | | | | + | | | U | | = | | U | | | | |
| 8 | 22 | 13 | 26 | | 14 | 6 | 15 | 12 | | 8 | 15 | 1 | 8 | 6 | 12 |

| | | | | | | | | | | | | | | | |
|---|---|---|---|---|---|---|---|---|---|---|---|---|---|---|---|
| | | | | | | | | | | | | | | | |
| 21 | 4 | 5 | | 10 | 18 | 13 | 17 | | 16 | 4 | 6 | 4 | 15 | 1 | 7 |

| | | | | | | | | | | | | | | | | |
|---|---|---|---|---|---|---|---|---|---|---|---|---|---|---|---|---|
| | | | | | | | | | | | | | | | | ? |
| 18 | 1 | 12 | | 22 | 13 | | 18 | | 1 | 18 | 22 | 13 | 14 | 4 | 5 | |

Play the game in groups of four. You will need a deck of playing cards. Each student gets six cards. Take turns asking for a card. For example: "Have you got the six of spades?" If you have it, say "Yes, I have" and give the card. If you don't have it, say, "No, I haven't". If you ask and don't get the card, draw one card from the deck. Once you have a set, put it down in front of you.

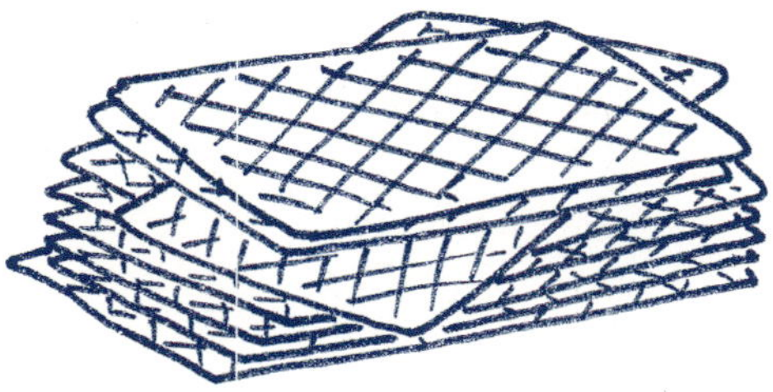

*Deck of playing cards*

*The six of spades*

*A set: the nine of clubs, hearts, diamonds and spades*

*A set: the king of hearts, spades, clubs and diamonds*

Then draw four new cards from the deck. The game is over when the deck is gone, or the lesson is over. The student with the most groups of four cards is the winner!

*The seven of spades*

*The jack of diamonds*

*The queen of clubs*

*The king of hearts*

*The ace of spades*

*Vier Schüler pro Gruppe. Ihr braucht ein Kartenspiel. Jede/r Schüler/in bekommt sechs Karten. Fragt abwechselnd nach bestimmten Karten. Z.B. „Hast du die Pik sechs?“ Wenn du die Karte hast, sag „Yes, I have“ und übergib die Karte. Wenn du sie nicht hast, sag „No, I haven't“.*

*Wenn du fragst und keine Karte bekommst, nimm eine Karte vom Stapel. Sobald du ein Set von vier Karten hast, leg sie vor dich hin. Dann nimm vier neue Karten vom Stapel. Das Spiel ist zu Ende, wenn alle Karten gezogen wurden, oder die Stunde vorbei ist. Der Schüler mit den meisten Sets von vier Karten gewinnt.*

# Unit 2 – Überblick

## KV 2.1 Match the verbs

In dieser Verb-Übung ordnen die Schüler zunächst den deutschen die englischen Infinitive zu und üben dann die Bildung des *simple present*, indem sie die dritte Person Singular bilden und aufschreiben.

## KV 2.2 Michael's school day

Anhand der Beschreibung eines Tagesablaufs übt diese KV sowohl die Versprachlichung der Uhrzeiten als auch die Bildung der dritten Person Singular des *simple present.*

## KV 2.3 Family cryptogram

Dieses Kryptogramm vertieft die „Familienwörter" sowie die Verwandtschaftsgrade. Wenn die Schüler einige Buchstaben eingefüllt haben, das ganze Wort aber noch nicht sehen, können sie durch den Sinn des Satzes vielleicht schon das Wort erkennen.

## KV 2.4 Scrambled family words

In dieser Aufgabe üben die S diverse „Familienwörter", indem sie die Buchstaben der einzelnen Wörter in die richtige Reihenfolge bringen. Die nummerierten Buchstaben ergeben eine Lösungsfrage.

## KV 2.5 Maggie's family tree

Hier üben die S ihr Leseverstehen während sie anhand kurzer Beschreibungen Maggies Stammbaum ausfüllen. Die einzelnen Sätze schildern die Verwandtschaftsgrade in Maggies Familie in ungeordneter Reihenfolge, sodass die S dazu gezwungen sind, die einzelnen Sätze genau zu lesen, um den Stammbaum zu vervollständigen.

## KV 2.6 Pet shop ads

Für diese Lückentextaufgabe müssen die S das passende Wort aus einem „Wortsäckchen" heraussuchen. So ist diese KV für lernschwächere S gut geeignet, eine Steigerung ist aber für lernstärkere S durch Abdecken der Wortsäckchen möglich. Nachdem sie den Lückentext ausgefüllt haben, können lernstärkere S auch anhand der Mustersätze auf der KV ihre eigenen Kurztexte über Haustiere schreiben.

## KV 2.7 Home sweet home

Die S suchen in dem Kreuzworträtsel Wörter zum Thema Zimmer und Möbel. Die grauen Nummern ergeben als Lösung den Spruch "There is no place like home."

*Match the German and English infinitives and write down the 3rd person singular.*

*Ordne die deutschen den englischen Infinitiven zu, und schreib die* dritte Person Singular.

| German infinitive | English infinitive | he, she, it |
|---|---|---|
| (sich) anziehen | to have a shower | |
| aufstehen | to read | |
| beobachten | to clean | |
| (sich) duschen | to do | |
| erzählen | to get up | gets up |
| essen | to sleep | |
| füttern | to drink | |
| geben | to write | |
| kommen | to put | |
| lesen | to get dressed | gets dressed |
| machen | to feed | |
| passen | to argue | |
| putzen | to wash | |
| schlafen | to wear | |
| schreiben | to fit | |
| stellen | to watch | |
| (sich) streiten | to give | |
| tragen | to eat | |
| trinken | to come | |
| (sich) waschen | to tell | |

# KV Michael's school day

*Complete the sentences about Michael's day.*

*Vervollständige die Sätze über Michaels Tag.*

get up

*Michael gets up at ten past seven in the morning.*

have a shower

*He has a shower at quarter past seven.*

have breakfast

______________________

take the bus[1]

______________________

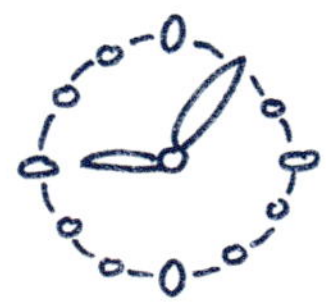

is at school

______________________

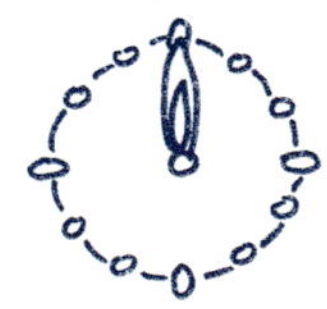

have lunch

______________________

come home

______________________

do his homework

______________________

play football

______________________

eat with his family

______________________

play computer games

______________________

go to bed

______________________

[1] take the bus = den Bus nehmen

*Match the letters and the numbers.*

*Ordne die Zahlen den Buchstaben zu.*

| A | B | C | D | E | F | G | H | I | J | K | L | M | N | O | P | Q | R | S | T | U | V | W | X | Y | Z |
|---|---|---|---|---|---|---|---|---|---|---|---|---|---|---|---|---|---|---|---|---|---|---|---|---|---|
| | | | | 7 | X | | | | X | X | | | 1 | | | X | | | | | X | X | X | X | X |

My grandparents are my

| | | | | | | | | | | | | | | | |
|---|---|---|---|---|---|---|---|---|---|---|---|---|---|---|---|
| | A | | | | T | | ’ | | | A | | | | T | |
| 11 | 10 | 24 | 7 | 1 | 5 | 13 | | | 11 | 10 | 24 | 7 | 1 | 5 | 13 |

My mother is my

| | | | | | | | | | | | | | | | | | | | | | |
|---|---|---|---|---|---|---|---|---|---|---|---|---|---|---|---|---|---|---|---|---|---|
| G | | A | | | | | | | | T | | ’ | | | A | | G | | T | | |
| 26 | 24 | 10 | 1 | 19 | 11 | 10 | 24 | 7 | 1 | 5 | 13 | | | 19 | 10 | 14 | 26 | 2 | 5 | 7 | 24 |

My uncle is my

| | | | | | | | | | | | | | | | |
|---|---|---|---|---|---|---|---|---|---|---|---|---|---|---|---|
| | | T | | | | ’ | | | | | | T | | | |
| 12 | 20 | 5 | 2 | 7 | 24 | | 13 | | 3 | 24 | 20 | 5 | 2 | 7 | 24 |

My aunt is my

| | | | | | | | | | | | | | | |
|---|---|---|---|---|---|---|---|---|---|---|---|---|---|---|
| | | T | | | | ’ | | | | | | T | | |
| 12 | 20 | 5 | 2 | 7 | 24 | | 13 | | 13 | 4 | 13 | 5 | 7 | 24 |

My cousins are my

| | | | | | | | | | | | | | | | | | | | | | | | | |
|---|---|---|---|---|---|---|---|---|---|---|---|---|---|---|---|---|---|---|---|---|---|---|---|---|
| A | | | T | | A | | | | | | | | | ’ | | | | | | | | | | |
| 10 | 14 | 1 | 5 | | 10 | 1 | 19 | | 14 | 1 | 16 | 21 | 7 | | 13 | | 16 | 2 | 4 | 21 | 19 | 24 | 7 | 1 |

I am my

| | | | | | | | | | | | | | | | | | | | | | | | |
|---|---|---|---|---|---|---|---|---|---|---|---|---|---|---|---|---|---|---|---|---|---|---|---|
| G | | A | | | | A | | | | T | | ’ | | G | | A | | | | | | | |
| 26 | 24 | 10 | 1 | 19 | 11 | 10 | 24 | 7 | 1 | 5 | 13 | | | 26 | 24 | 10 | 1 | 19 | 16 | 2 | 4 | 21 | 19 |

My brother and I are my

| | | | | | | | | | | | | | | | | |
|---|---|---|---|---|---|---|---|---|---|---|---|---|---|---|---|---|
| | A | | | | T | | ’ | | | | | | | | | |
| 11 | 10 | 24 | 7 | 1 | 5 | 13 | | | 16 | 2 | 4 | 21 | 19 | 24 | 7 | 1 |

# KV Scrambled family words

*Write the unscrambled words in the boxes. Then write the numbered letters below and answer the question.*

*Schreibe die entwirrten Wörter in die Kästchen. Dann schreib die nummerierten Buchstaben darunter und beantworte die Frage.*

| | | | | | | | | | | |
|---|---|---|---|---|---|---|---|---|---|---|
| FTHAER | 8 | | | | | | | | | |
| GCHIRANDLD | | | | | | | | | 12 | |
| ANUT | 14 | | | | | | | | | |
| NSO | | | 13 | | | | | | | |
| MHTOER | 10 | | | | | | | | | |
| GRPAAND | | | 2 | | | | | | | |
| DUGATHER | | | | | | | 16 | | | |
| BRTHEOR | | | 5 | | | | | | | |
| GRDNAMA | | 7 | | | | 15 | 9 | | | |
| ULCNE | 6 | | | | | | | | | |
| PREANTS | | | | | | 3 | | | | |
| SSTIER | | | 4 | | | | | | | |
| CSUOIN | | | | | 11 | | | | | |
| CLHID | | 1 | | | | | | | | |

W _ _ _ ' _ y _ _ _ _ _ _ _ _ y _ _ _ _ ?

1 2 3 4 5 6 7 8 9 10 11 12 13 14 15 16

*Fill in Maggie's family tree.*

*Vervollständige Maggies Familienstammbaum.*

- Maggie has got a brother. His name is Luke.
- Aunt Rebecca is married to Uncle Alex. They have got a son. His name is Ben. Ben is one of Maggie's cousins.
- Maggie has got four grandparents. Her father's parents are Grandma and Grandpa Clark. Her mother's parents are Grandma and Grandpa Harris.
- Maggie's parents are Jane and Henry, but Maggie says mum and dad to them.
- Maggie's mother has got a sister. Her name is Rebecca.
- Maggie's father Henry has got a sister and a brother. Their names are Hannah and George.
- Uncle George is married to Aunt Liz. They have got two children, a son and a daughter. Their names are Jessica and Sam. Jessica and Sam are two of Maggie's cousins.

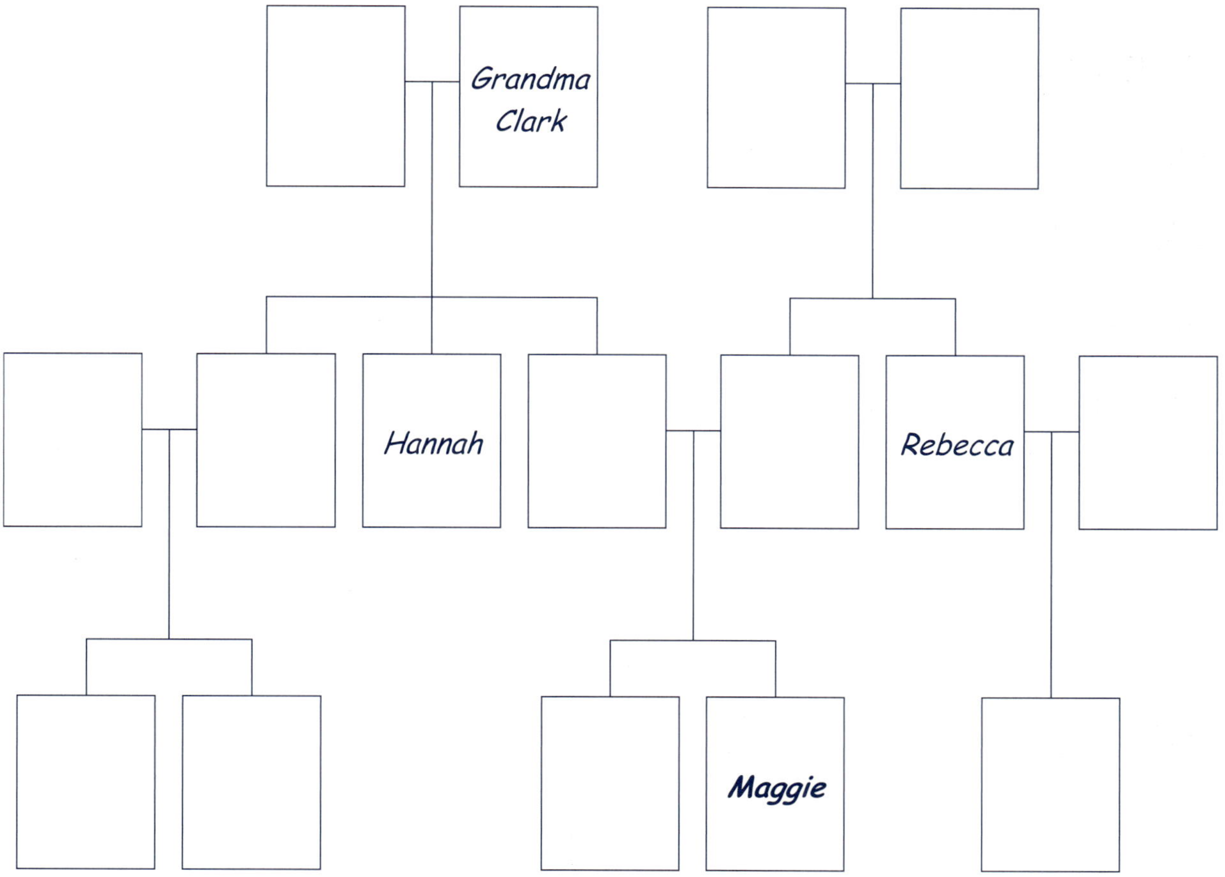

# 2.6 KV Pet shop ads

*The ads for this pet shop are missing some words. Can you help? Fill in the missing words below. Use the words from the word bags.*

*Den Anzeigen für diese Tierhandlung fehlen einige Wörter. Kannst du helfen? Ergänze die fehlenden Wörter. Benutze die Wörter in den Wortsäckchen.*

This is ___Pete___ the ___rabbit___.

Pete eats ____________ and drinks ____________.

He ____________ in a hutch.

Pete ____________ like milk.

He ____________ small black eyes.

*Pete*

This is ____________ the ____________.

Bobby is two ____________.

He doesn't ____________ songs.

Bobby lives in a ____________.

He is green, ____________ and ____________.

*Bobby*

*Carlos*

This is ____________ the ____________.

Carlos likes ____________.

He sleeps in a ____________.

Carlos is ____________ and ____________.

He ____________ a nice family.

*Fill in the crossword and find the phrase.*

*Löse das Kreuzworträtsel und finde den Lösungssatz.*

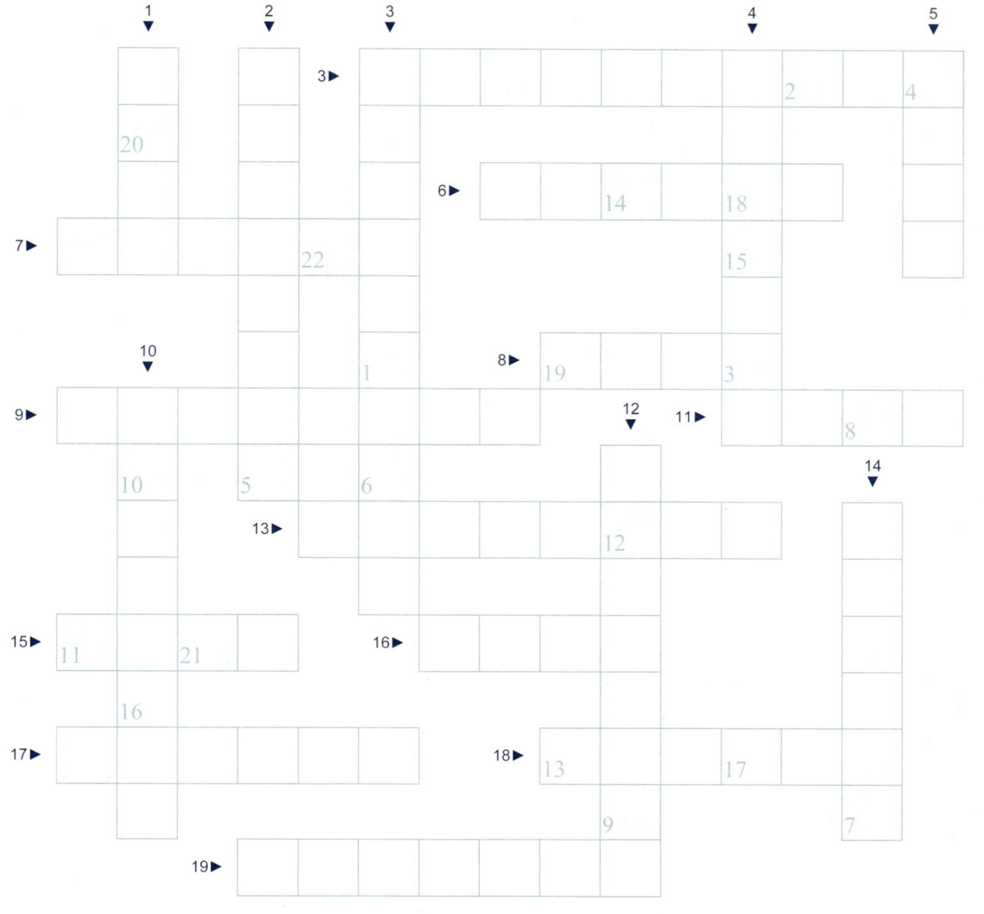

**Across:**

| | |
|---|---|
| 3 | Geschirrspülmaschine |
| 6 | Stereoanlage |
| 7 | Garten |
| 8 | Heim, Zuhause |
| 9 | Schrank |
| 11 | Spüle, Spülbecken |
| 13 | Sessel |
| 15 | Lampe |
| 16 | Badewanne |
| 17 | Kühlschrank |
| 18 | Herd |
| 19 | Schlafzimmer |

**Down:**

| | |
|---|---|
| 1 | Sofa |
| 2 | Kleiderschrank |
| 3 | unten; nach unten |
| 4 | Regale |
| 5 | Raum, Zimmer |
| 10 | oben; nach oben |
| 12 | Badezimmer |
| 14 | Treppe; Treppenstufen |

___ ___ ___ ___ ___ (1 2 3 4 5)  ___ ___ (6 7)  ___ ___ (8 9)

___ ___ ___ ___ ___ (10 11 12 13 14)  ___ ___ ___ ___ (15 16 17 18)  ___ ___ ___ ___! (19 20 21 22)

# Unit 3 – Überblick

## KV 3.1 Sports quiz
Diese Aufgabe übt sowohl die Verneinung einfacher Sätze im *simple present* als auch Wortschatz zum Thema Sport und Hobbys.

## KV 3.2 Laura's bedroom & Where are Laura's clothes?
Die Kopiervorlagen zu "Laura's bedroom" üben Wortschatz zu den Wortfeldern Kleidung und Möbel, sowie die Präpositionen *on, in* und *under*. Für lernschwächere S kann L zu der Frage *"Where are Laura's clothes?"* zusätzlich noch Möbelwortschatz wie z. B. *armchair, bed, chair, desk, sofa* und *wardrobe* an die Tafel schreiben.

## KV 3.3 Opposites
In dieser Aufgabe ordnen die S häufig verwendete Gegensatzpaare einander zu. Die S benötigen eine Schere, um die einzelnen Dreiecke auszuschneiden. Die Kante des Rhombus ist mit Schwarz abgegrenzt, sodass die S einen Ansatzpunkt zum Wiederzusammenbasteln haben.

## KV 3.4 Shopping
Diese KV übt sowohl den Wortschatz zum Thema *Shopping* als auch das Leseverstehen der S. Für diese Aufgabe benötigen die S eine Schere, um die Sätze auszuschneiden. Die Sätze sind teilweise nummeriert, sodass die S ein Ansatzpunkt haben.

## KV 3.5 Pounds and pence, euros and cents
In dieser Übung verbinden die S die gesprochenen Preise mit den geschriebenen. Eine Steigerung ist dadurch möglich, dass die S nur die eine oder andere Hälfte der KV bekommen, und die Preisangaben der jeweils fehlenden Seite eigenständig aufschreiben. Die Ergebnisse können die S dann in Partnerarbeit vergleichen.

## KV 3.6 Michael's week
Die Häufigkeitsadverben und das Schreiben einfacher Satze im *simple present* sind Thema dieser KV. Die Schüler entnehmen der Tabelle, wie oft in der Woche Michael etwas Bestimmtes macht, und schreiben dazu jeweils einen Satz.

## KV 3.7 Maggie visits her grandparents
Dieser Lückentext übt sowohl die Fragewörter *who, what, where* und *when* als auch das Leseverstehen der S. Die S müssen – ausgehend vom jeweils vorhergehenden Satz und mithilfe der Antworten Maggies – herausfinden, welches Fragewort sie in die Lücken einsetzen sollen.

*Can you figure out the name of the sport from each picture? Then write one positive and one negative sentence about each sport.*

*Kannst du den Namen der Sportart aus den Bildern erraten? Dann schreib einen positiven und einen negativen Satz über jede Sportart.*

1. *I play basketball.*

   *I don't play basketball.*

2. ______________________________

   ______________________________

3. ______________________________

   ______________________________

4. ______________________________

   ______________________________

5. ______________________________

   ______________________________

6. ______________________________

   ______________________________

7. ______________________________

   ______________________________

# KV Laura's bedroom

*Laura always makes a mess in her bedroom! Can you help clean it up? Unscramble the words and match them with the clothes on the floor.*

*In Lauras Zimmer herrscht immer Unordnung! Kannst du beim Aufräumen helfen? Entwirre die Wörter und ordne sie den Sachen auf dem Boden zu.*

**1.** SSGALUNSES SUNGLASSES

**2.** SKCOS ____________

**3.** T-ISRHT ____________

**4.** BOTOS ____________

**5.** STORHS ____________

**6.** SRIHT ____________

**7.** JANES ____________

**8.** SEAWTSIRHT ____________

**9.** DSERS ____________

**10.** SOEHS ____________

**11.** FTOLOLABL BTOOS ____________

*Write where Laura's clothes are in the room. Use the prepositions* on, in *and* under.

*Schreib, wo Lauras Sachen in ihrem Zimmer sind. Benutze die Präpositionen* on, in *und* under.

*Her sunglasses are on the desk.*

# 3.3 KV Opposites

*The pairs of opposites are all mixed up! Cut out the triangles and find the pairs.*

*Die Gegensatzpaare sind durcheinander geraten! Schneide die Dreiecke aus und finde die Paare.*

*Amy and her mum are looking for a dress for her grandfather's 75th birthday party, but Amy only likes jeans. Cut out the sentences and put them in the right order.*

*Amy und ihre Mutter suchen ein Kleid für den 75. Geburtstag ihres Großvaters, aber Amy mag nur Jeans. Schneide die Sätze aus und bring sie in die richtige Reihenfolge.*

| | | |
|---|---|---|
| | **Mrs Graham:** | Maybe. Your favourite colours are red and blue, right? What about that dress? |
| | **Shop Assistant:** | Does it fit? |
| 15 | **Amy:** | Sorry. Now can we look for jeans? |
| | **Mrs Graham:** | Amy! We'll take it, and thank you very much for your help. |
| | **Shop Assistant:** | OK. Here you are, a size M blue and green dress. |
| 5 | **Amy:** | Well, OK. But can I have new jeans too? |
| 9 | **Mrs Graham:** | Thank you. Try it on, Amy. |
| 11 | **Amy:** | Yes, the dress fits. |
| 1 | **Shop Assistant:** | Good morning. Can I help you? |
| 13 | **Amy:** | No, I don't like the dress, but I have to wear it anyway. |
| 3 | **Amy:** | Mum, do I have to wear a dress? I hate dresses. |
| | **Mrs Graham:** | Yes, please. We need a new dress for my daughter. Size M, please. |
| | **Mrs Graham:** | Yes, you have to wear a dress. I'm sorry Amy. You can't wear your jeans to your grandfather's 75th birthday party. |
| 7 | **Amy:** | No, I don't like red and blue, I like blue and green. |
| | **Shop Assistant:** | Do you like it? |

# KV Pounds and pence, euros and cents

*Match how we say a price with how we write it.*

*Verbinde die gesprochenen Preise mit den geschriebenen.*

sixteen euros forty-seven cents

one pound

seventy-nine cents

three pounds seventy-five p

one pound ninety-nine p

nine pounds sixty-five p

two-hundred thirty-three pounds fifty p

five euros ninety-six cents

fifty p

six pounds thirty-seven p

eighty-three p

thirty-four pounds twenty-one p

two euros eighty-seven cents

83p

€0.79

€2.87

£233.50

£9.65

€5.96

£1

£6.37

£3.75

€16.47

£34.21

50p

£1.99

*Answer the questions about Michael's week.*

*Beantworte die Fragen zu Michaels Woche.*

How often[1] does Michael …

| | | Monday | Tuesday | Wednesday | Thursday | Friday | Saturday | Sunday |
|---|---|---|---|---|---|---|---|---|
| 1 | have a shower? | ✓ | ✓ | ✓ | ✓ | ✓ | ✓ | ✓ |
| 2 | read comics with his brother? | | | | | | ✓ | ✓ |
| 3 | do homework? | ✓ | ✓ | ✓ | ✓ | ✓ | | |
| 4 | play football? | ✓ | | ✓ | | ✓ | | ✓ |
| 5 | lay the table? | | ✓ | | ✓ | ✓ | ✓ | ✓ |
| 6 | play the guitar? | | | | | | | |
| 7 | feed his rabbit? | ✓ | ✓ | ✓ | ✓ | ✓ | ✓ | ✓ |
| 8 | play hockey? | ✓ | | ✓ | | | ✓ | |
| 9 | collect stamps? | | | | | | | |
| 10 | listen to a CD? | | | | | | ✓ | ✓ |

1. *Michael always has a shower.* ______
2. *Michael sometimes reads comics with his brother.* ______
3. ______
4. ______
5. ______
6. ______
7. ______
8. ______
9. ______
10. ______

*never = 0 times a week[2]*
*sometimes = 2 times a week*
*often = 3 or 4 times a week*
*usually = 5 times a week*
*always = 7 times a week*

[1] How often? = Wie oft?
[2] times a week = mal in der Woche

# KV Maggie visits her grandparents

*Maggie visits her grandparents Grandma and Grandpa Clark at the weekend. They ask lots of questions, but can't hear very well. Fill in the missing question words* who, what, where *or* when.

*Maggie besucht ihre Großeltern Grandma und Grandpa Clark über das Wochenende. Sie stellen viele Fragen, können aber Maggie nicht sehr gut hören. Füll die Lücken mit den richtigen Fragewörtern* who, what, where *oder* when.

**Grandpa Clark:** Well Maggie, how is school?

**Maggie:** OK. I have to get up very early in the morning for school. I don't like that.

**Grandma Clark:** ___What___ do you have to do in the morning?

**Maggie:** Get up very early for school. Usually at half past six in the morning.

**Grandpa Clark:** ___When___ do you get up in the morning?

**Maggie:** At half past six. Then I have breakfast downstairs with Luke and mum.

**Grandma Clark:** ______________ do you have breakfast?

**Maggie:** Downstairs. After that I often have to run, because Luke is very slow[1].

**Grandpa Clark:** ______________ is slow?

**Maggie:** Luke. He takes a shower for an hour in the mornings. Then we walk together to school.

**Grandma Clark:** ______________ does Luke take a shower for an hour?

**Maggie:** In the mornings. I think he is always late because he really doesn't like school.

**Grandpa Clark:** ______________ does Luke not like?

**Maggie:** School. But I think it's OK. My favourite subject is German.

**Grandma Clark:** ______________ is your favourite subject?

**Maggie:** German. We've got German on Mondays, Wednesdays and Fridays.

**Grandpa Clark:** ______________ have you got German class?

**Maggie:** On Mondays, Wednesdays and Fridays. My German teacher is Frau Schneider. She's really nice.

**Grandma Clark:** ______________ is your teacher?

**Maggie:** Frau Schneider. She's from Cologne, in Germany.

**Grandpa Clark:** ______________ is she from?

**Maggie:** Cologne. It's in Germany. But enough about me. How are you?[2]

[1] slow = langsam
[2] But enough about me. How are you? = Aber genug von mir. Wie geht es euch?

# Unit 4 – Überblick

## KV 4.1 Birthday invitation

Mit dieser KV werden Wortschatz zum Thema Party sowie das Leseverstehen der S geübt. Dieses Kryptogramm ist etwas komplizierter als die vorherigen, da eine ganze Email codiert ist.

## KV 4.2 At Sarah's party

Das *present progressive* und das Leseverstehen der S werden hier geübt. Das Thema Party wird auch in dieser Aufgabe weitergeführt. Grundidee: Sarahs Party wird aus der Sicht von Sarahs jüngerem Geschwisterkind geschildert. Dieses beobachtet die Ereignisse, die sich auf der Party abspielen, und berichtet einer Freundin am Telefon darüber.

## KV 4.3 A bottle of ...

Diese KV übt Wortschatz zum Thema Lebensmittel und den jeweils unterschiedlichen Behältnissen/Verpackungen oder Darreichungsformen. Die S können anhand der Bilder die passenden Behältnisse heraussuchen und aufschreiben.

## KV 4.4 My body

Diese Aufgabe übt Wortschatz zum Thema Körper. Die S schreiben zunächst die Körperteile unter das richtige *group word*. Dann beschriften sie die Bilder und festigen dabei den Wortschatz weiter.

## KV 4.5 *Some* or *any*?

Diese KV übt die Verwendung von *some* und *any* und auch das Schreiben einfacher positiver und negativer Aussagesätze im *simple present*.

## KV 4.6 Personal pronouns

Die Personalpronomen stehen im Mittelpunkt dieser KV. In 20 Satzpaaren üben die S das Zusammenspiel von Substantiv und Personalpronomen, wobei der jeweils erste Satz Anhaltspunkte zur Füllung der Lücke im zweiten Satz liefert.

## KV 4.7 Funny food

Diese KV übt sowohl den neuen Wortschatz als auch das Schreiben kurzer Dialoge zum Thema Essen. Dabei werden sowohl die Fragebildung (*Would you like ...?*) als auch verneinte Kurzantworten und positive Aussagen (*I'd like ...*) gefestigt. Die S müssen in dieser Übung die richtige Kombination der Esswaren aufschreiben, indem sie die unterstrichenen Wörter durch Wörter aus dem Kasten ersetzen.

*Sarah's e-mail to her friends got all messed up. Can you help?*

*Sarahs E-Mail zu ihren Freunden ist durcheinander gekommen. Kannst du helfen?*

| A | B | C | D | E | F | G | H | I | J | K | L | M | N | O | P | Q | R | S | T | U | V | W | X | Y | Z |
|---|---|---|---|---|---|---|---|---|---|---|---|---|---|---|---|---|---|---|---|---|---|---|---|---|---|
| | | | | | | | | | X | | | | | | | X | | | | | | | X | | X |

| D | E | A | R | | C | L | A | S | S | M | A | T | E | S | , |
|---|---|---|---|---|---|---|---|---|---|---|---|---|---|---|---|
| 5 | 22 | 11 | 12 | | 10 | 14 | 11 | 17 | 17 | 3 | 11 | 8 | 22 | 17 | |

| | | | | | | | | | | | | | | | | | | | | | | |
|---|---|---|---|---|---|---|---|---|---|---|---|---|---|---|---|---|---|---|---|---|---|---|
| | | | | | | | | | | | | | | | | | | | | | | |
| 18 | | 16 | 11 | 24 | 8 | | 8 | 26 | | 18 | 24 | 4 | 18 | 8 | 22 | | 2 | 26 | 1 | | 8 | 26 |

| | | | | | | | | | | | | | | | | | | | | | |
|---|---|---|---|---|---|---|---|---|---|---|---|---|---|---|---|---|---|---|---|---|---|
| | | | | | | | | | | | | | | | | | . | | | | |
| 3 | 2 | | 19 | 18 | 12 | 8 | 13 | 5 | 11 | 2 | | 7 | 11 | 12 | 8 | 2 | | | 8 | 13 | 22 |

| | | | | | | | | | | | | | | | | | | | | |
|---|---|---|---|---|---|---|---|---|---|---|---|---|---|---|---|---|---|---|---|---|
| | | | | | | | | | | | | | | | | | | | | |
| 7 | 11 | 12 | 8 | 2 | | 17 | 8 | 11 | 12 | 8 | 17 | | 11 | 8 | | 8 | 13 | 12 | 22 | 22 |

| | | | | | | | | | | | | | | | | | | |
|---|---|---|---|---|---|---|---|---|---|---|---|---|---|---|---|---|---|---|
| | ' | | | | | | | | | | | | | | | | | |
| 26 | | 10 | 14 | 26 | 10 | 20 | | 26 | 24 | | 17 | 11 | 8 | 1 | 12 | 5 | 11 | 2 |

| | | | | | | | | | | | | | | | | | |
|---|---|---|---|---|---|---|---|---|---|---|---|---|---|---|---|---|---|
| | | | | | | | | | . | | | | | | | | |
| 11 | 15 | 8 | 22 | 12 | 24 | 26 | 26 | 24 | | | 18 | 8 | | 18 | 17 | | 11 |

| | | | | | | | | | | | | | | | | | | | |
|---|---|---|---|---|---|---|---|---|---|---|---|---|---|---|---|---|---|---|---|
| | | | | | - | | | | | | | | | | | | , | | | |
| 15 | 11 | 24 | 10 | 2 | | 5 | 12 | 22 | 17 | 17 | | 7 | 11 | 12 | 8 | 2 | | | 17 | 26 |

| | | | | | | | | | | | | | | | | |
|---|---|---|---|---|---|---|---|---|---|---|---|---|---|---|---|---|
| | | | | | | | | | | | | | | | | |
| 7 | 14 | 22 | 11 | 17 | 22 | | 16 | 22 | 11 | 12 | | 15 | 1 | 24 | 24 | 2 |

| | | | | | | | | | | | | | | | | | | | |
|---|---|---|---|---|---|---|---|---|---|---|---|---|---|---|---|---|---|---|---|
| | | | | | | | ! | | | | | | | | | | | | |
| 10 | 14 | 26 | 8 | 13 | 22 | 17 | | | 18 | | 11 | 3 | | 3 | 11 | 20 | 18 | 24 | 25 |

| | | | | | | | | | | | | | | | | |
|---|---|---|---|---|---|---|---|---|---|---|---|---|---|---|---|---|
| | | | | | | | | | | | , | | | | | ! |
| 14 | 26 | 8 | 17 | | 26 | 15 | | 15 | 26 | 26 | 5 | | | 3 | 3 | 3 | |

| | | | | | | | | | | | | |
|---|---|---|---|---|---|---|---|---|---|---|---|---|
| | | | | | | | | | | | | ! |
| 17 | 22 | 22 | | 2 | 26 | 1 | | 8 | 13 | 22 | 24 | |

| | | | | |
|---|---|---|---|---|
| | | | | |
| 17 | 11 | 12 | 11 | 13 |

*You are Sarah's younger brother or sister, but you haven't got an invitation to Sarah's birthday party. You want to watch what is happening anyway. Your friend Julia is on the phone. She wants to know about the party too. Complete the sentences with the correct form of the* present progressive.

*Du bist Sarahs jüngere/r Schwester/Bruder, aber du hast keine Einladung zu ihrer Geburtstagsparty bekommen. Du willst trotzdem sehen, was passiert. Du telefonierst gerade mit deiner Freundin Julia. Sie möchte auch wissen, was auf der Party passiert. Vervollständige die Sätze mit der korrekten Verbform im* present progressive.

Hi Julia! I _'m watching_______ (watch) Sarah get ready for her birthday party right now.

No, I haven't got an invitation, so I _'m not going_______ (not go) to the party. Shh! I hear a

noise! Sarah's guests ______________________ (come) to her door and

______________________ (ring) her doorbell. Sarah ______________________ (open) the

door, and now all of her friends ______________________ (say)

"Happy birthday" to her. She ______________________ (take) all of their presents.

There are a lot of guests, so there are a lot of presents too. I want some of her presents!

Sarah ______________________ (put) all of her presents on the table.

Now she ______________________ (invite) all of her guests into the living room.

She ______________________ (put) some music in the CD player and

______________________ (pass) round lots of party food. The food looks great. John

______________________ (eat) chicken and chips, and Stacey ______________________

(drink) some lemonade. There's cake and ice cream too! Now Sarah ______________________

(open) her presents. She is really happy about her new CD, sunglasses and books. Everyone wants to go

outside and play some party games, so they ______________________ (leave[1]) the living room.

Fantastic! Now I ______________________ (eat) some of the cake and ice cream!

[1] leave = verlassen

# 4.3 KV A bottle of ...

*How do you eat? Complete the sentences by using the pictures below.*

*Wie isst du? Vervollständige die Sätze mit Hilfe der Bilder.*

**1.** I eat lunch and dinner on a _________________________.

**2.** I always eat my cornflakes out of a _________________________.

**3.** You buy milk from the shop in a _________________________.

**4.** Eight glasses of juice fit into a _________________________.

**5.** A _________________________ of crisps is not very expensive.

**6.** You cut up a big pizza into lots of _________________________

so that everyone gets some.

**7.** Your mum says "Don't drink the milk out of the

_________________________, drink it out of a

_________________________."

**8.** Apples, oranges and bananas are usually in a big

_________________________.

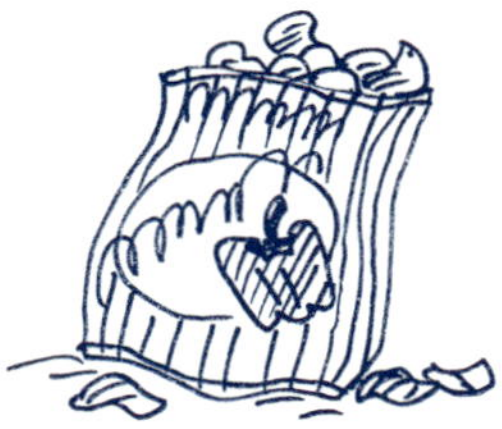

*Write the body parts under the correct group word. Then label the pictures.*

*Schreib die Körperteile unter den richtigen Oberbegriff. Beschrifte dann die Bilder.*

| **arm** | **leg** | **head** | |
|---|---|---|---|
| ______ | ______ | ______ | ______ |
| ______ | ______ | ______ | ______ |
| ______ | ______ | ______ | ______ |
| | | | ______ |

face · shoulder · mouth · hand · knee · ear · eye · foot/feet · finger/fingers · tooth/teeth · hair · nose · toe/toes

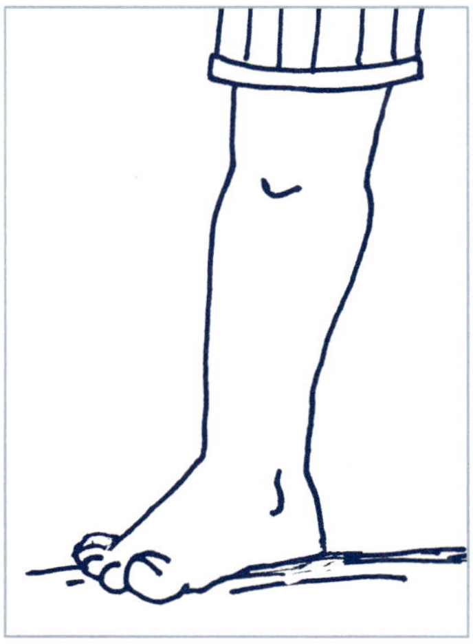

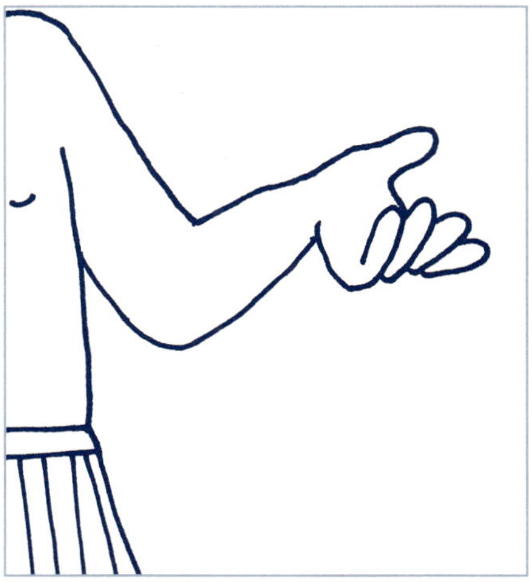

# KV Some or any?

*Fill in* some *or* any *in the … spaces, then answer the questions with yes and no.*

*Fülle* some *oder* any *in die … Lücken, dann beantworte die Fragen einmal mit ja und einmal mit nein.*

**1.** Have you got ……*any*…… British money at home?

*Yes, I've got some British money at home.*

*No, I haven't got any British money at home.*

**2.** Do you need ………….. pens or pencils for school?

**3.** Have you got ………….. photos of friends in your room?

**4.** Would you like ………….. new books?

**5.** Have you got ………….. computer games?

**6.** Are there ………….. lamps in your room?

**7.** Have you got ………….. food in your room?

*Fill in the blanks with the correct personal pronoun.*

*Vervollständige die Sätze mit den richtigen Personalpronomen.*

me • you • him • her • it • us • you • them

1. Where's Mum? I can't see *her* ______.
2. I've got a new game. Would you like to play with *me* ______?
3. It's my birthday party next week. Would you like to come to ______?
4. I can't do my Maths homework. Can you help ______?
5. I can't find my football. Have you got ______?
6. We don't know what to do. Can you help ______?
7. Is John in the kitchen, Dad? I have to talk to ______.
8. Maggie! Luke! Where are you? There's a present for ______.
9. The twins are out. You have to wait for ______.
10. Grandma is at home. You can phone ______.
11. You can hear Tom, but he can't hear ______.
12. Those plates are very expensive. Don't drop ______.
13. Mrs Lane is a teacher. You have to listen to ______.
14. The fridge door is open. Can you close ______?
15. Why do you want to invite John? I don't like ______.
16. We are going shopping. Do you want to come with ______?
17. This exercise is very difficult. Can you help me with ______?
18. These glasses look bad. Please wash ______.
19. Hey, Dan. Where are you? I have to talk to ______.
20. Mmm, this chicken is very good. Try ______!

# KV Funny food

*Ann likes different food compared to most people. She wants to give you some food. Do you like it? What would you like to eat? The words in the box below will help you.*

*Ann mag anderes Essen als die meisten Leute. Sie möchte dir etwas zu essen geben. Magst du es? Was möchtest du essen? Die Wörter unten werden dir helfen.*

**1.** Would you like mints on your pizza?

*No, thank you. I'd like cheese on my pizza.*

**2.** Would you like orange juice on your cornflakes?

**3.** Would you like lasagne on your toast?

**4.** Would you like potatoes and sausages in your fruit salad?

**5.** Would you like ice cream with your chicken?

**6.** Would you like orange juice and cola in your hot chocolate?

**7.** Would you like fruit salad and cake in your sandwich?

apples • bananas • carrots • cheese • chocolate • marmalade
meat • milk • oranges • potatoes • roll • salad

# Unit 5 – Überblick

## KV 5.1 Did you …?

Diese Aufgabe übt das Ausformulieren von Notizen und den Gebrauch des *simple past* in positiven und negativen Aussagesätzen.

## KV 5.2 When I was your age …

Die S beschäftigen sich inhaltlich weiter mit dem Thema *school in the past*, indem sie diesen Lückentext mit der richtigen Form der vorgegebenen Verben im *simple past* vervollständigen.

## KV 5.3 What did Michael do yesterday?

Die S wiederholen das Verschriftlichen der Zeiten (siehe auch Unit 2) und üben das *simple past*. Als Steigerung des Schwierigkeitsgrades müssen sie jetzt aber zunächst erst die Zeiten bzw. Aktivitäten in die richtige Reihenfolge bringen. Leistungsstärkere S können zusätzlich Wörter wie *then, after, later* einfügen, um die Abfolge der Ereignisse fließender zu gestalten.

## KV 5.4 Match the verbs

Diese KV übt einige schwierigere Formen des *simple past* durch direkte Gegenüberstellung und ist daher gerade für lernschwächere Schüler gut geeignet.

## KV 5.5 Tangrams

Mithilfe dieses Tangram-Puzzles können die S die *simple past*-Formen regelmäßiger und unregelmäßiger Verben auf spielerische Art und Weise üben. Die S brauchen eine Schere, um die Puzzle auszuschneiden. Richtig zusammengestellt ergibt jedes der Ausgangs-Vierecke eine Form: entweder ein Tier oder einen Baum. Wenn die S Probleme haben, kann L die einzelnen Lösungs-Formen (Tannenbaum, sitzende Katze, Hase, stehende Katze und Gans) an die Tafel schreiben.

## KV 5.6 Letter mix

Im ersten Teil dieser Übung vergegenwärtigen sich die S anhand einer tabellarischen Gegenüberstellung den Unterschied zwischen *simple present, present progressive* und *simple past*. Im zweiten Teil wenden die S ihre Kenntnisse an, indem sie sich fünf Sätze im *simple past* ausdenken und aufschreiben.

## KV 5.7 Morris the tennis star

In dieser Aufgabe vervollständigen die S Interviewfragen mit *many* or *much* und üben dabei den Gebrauch dieser Mengenadverbien. Leistungsstärkere Schüler können danach die Antworten von Morris, dem interviewten Tennisstar, selbst erfinden, leistungsschwächere denken sich in Partnerarbeit die Antworten zusammen aus.

# Did you ...?

*Jane is doing a project for her class. She asked her mum about her old school and took notes about her answers. Now she needs to write full sentences. Can you help?*

*Jane macht ein Projekt für die Schule. Sie befragt ihre Mutter zu ihrer alten Schule und hat sich Notizen zu ihren Antworten gemacht. Jetzt muss sie die Sätze ausschreiben. Kannst du ihr helfen?*

| My questions | My notes | My mum's answers |
|---|---|---|
| 1) Did you use computers? | no, pen + paper | They didn't use computers, they used pen and paper. |
| 2) Did you have exercise books? | yes | They had exercise books. |
| 3) Did you learn English? | yes, + Latin + French | |
| 4) Did you listen to CDs and watch DVDs? | no | |
| 5) Did you talk in class? | yes, but only when the teacher said it was OK | |
| 6) Did you play in the classroom or outside in the breaks? | outside | |
| 7) Did the teachers help you when you had a question? | yes | |
| 8) Did you have P.E.? | yes, but mum ~~like~~ running | |
| 9) Did you drink water in the classroom? | no | |
| 10) Did you use books in class? | yes | |
| 11) Did you play after school in your free time? | yes | |
| 12) Did you like school? | yes, but mum liked summer holidays best | |

*Jane is doing a project for her class. She asked her grandpa about his old school and recorded the interview. Some words weren't recorded. Can you help by filling in the blanks?*

*Jane macht ein Projekt für die Schule. Sie hat ihren Großvater zu seiner alten Schule befragt und das Interview aufgenommen. Einige Wörter sind leider nicht aufgenommen worden. Kannst du helfen, indem du die Lücken füllst?*

So you want to hear about my school? Well Jane, when I *was* ________ (be) your age, school was very different from today. In the morning we *had to get up* ________ (have to get up) very early, then we ________________ (walk) for an hour to school. It ________________ (start) at seven o'clock and ________________ (finish) at four o'clock. We only ________________ (have) one break in the day at twelve o'clock, for lunch. We ________________ (have) lots of subjects that you have too, Jane, like History, French, German, Maths and Science. But we ________________ (~~have~~) Art, Music or Drama. There ________________ (be) both boys and girls in our class but we ________________ (have) to sit in different parts of the room. Our teacher ________________ (~~be~~) very nice and he often ________________ (shout) at us.

I ________________ (~~like~~) him. He always ________________ (tell) us to sit still.[1] We never ________________ (talk) to our friends in class and we ________________ (~~do~~) partner or group work. After school we ________________ (come) home again and then we ________________ (do) our homework. The homework ________________ (be) often very difficult. I usually ________________ (finish) at nine o'clock at night! So Jane, your school is great! Don't you think so too?

[1] sit still = sich ruhig verhalten

# What did Michael do yesterday?

*Put Michael's activities from yesterday in the right order. Then complete the sentences.*

*Bringe Michaels gestrige Aktivitäten in die richtige Reihenfolge. Vervollständige dann die Sätze.*

run for the bus[1]

play football

go to bed

sit in class

hurt[2] his foot

#1

get up

watch TV

be back home

#2

have breakfast

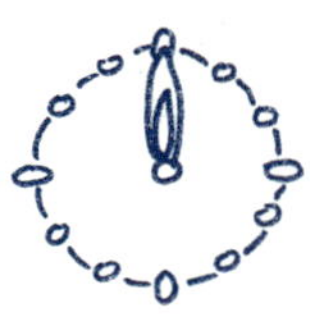
see his friends

do homework

make a model

*Michael got up at ten past seven in the morning. He had breakfast at quarter to eight.*

______________________________________________

______________________________________________

______________________________________________

______________________________________________

______________________________________________

[1] run for the bus = dem Bus hinterher laufen
[2] hurt = wehtun

*Match the infinitive with its* simple past *form by colouring the two petals the same colour.*

*Ordne die Infinitive den einfachen Formen der Vergangenheit zu, indem du die Blütenblätter in der gleichen Farbe ausmalst.*

*Tangrams are Chinese puzzles that you cut out and put back together to make different pictures. If you match the infinitive and the* simple past *form of the same verb you will see the picture!*

*Tangrams sind chinesische Puzzles, die man ausschneidet und wieder zusammensetzt, um verschiedene Bilder herzustellen. Wenn du den Infinitiv und die einfache Form der Vergangenheit zusammenfügst, siehst du ein Bild!*

**1.**

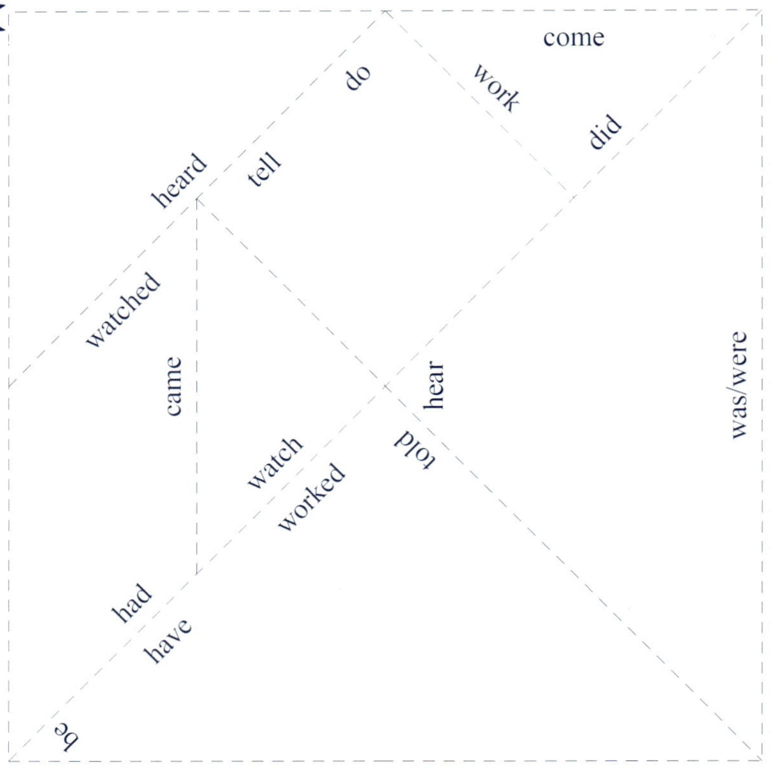


**2.**

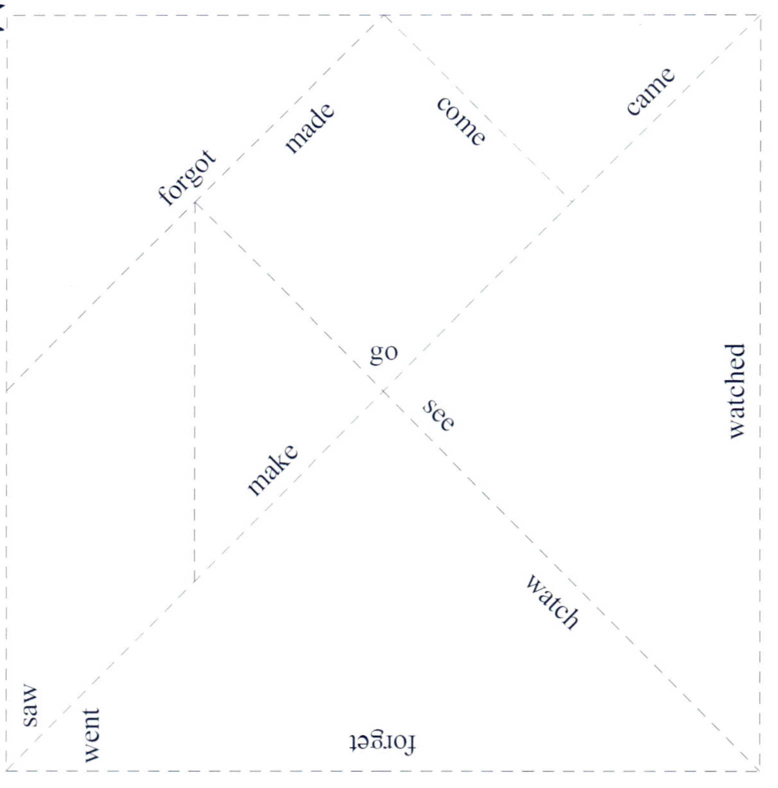

3.

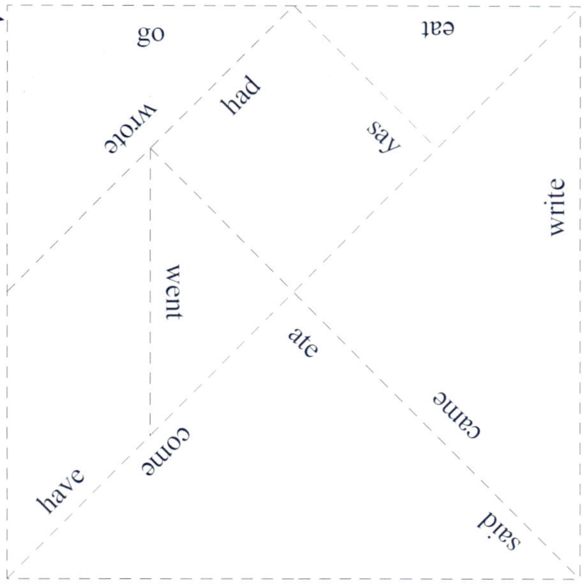
go
eat
wrote
had
say
write
went
ate
came
have
come
said

4.

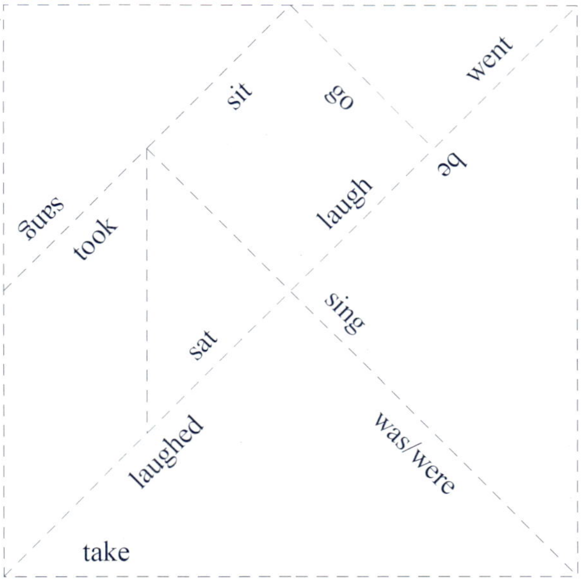
sit
go
went
be
sang
took
laugh
sing
sat
laughed
was/were
take

5.

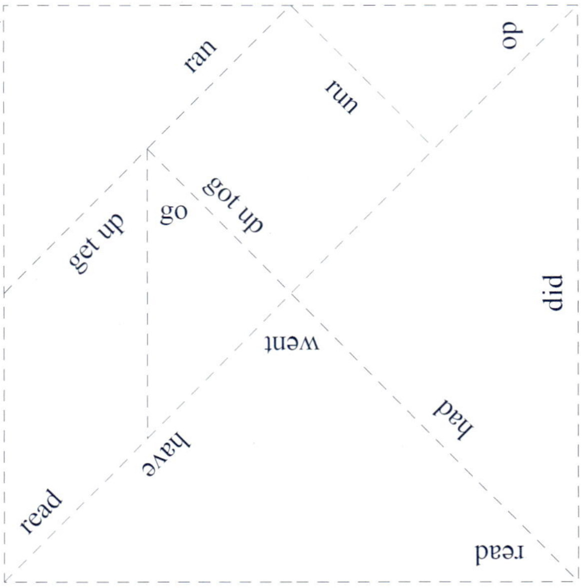
ran
run
do
get up
go
got up
did
went
had
have
read
read

# KV Letter mix

*Find fifteen verbs in this letter mix and write them down under the correct group word. Then write five sentences with these verbs.*

*Finde fünfzehn Verben im Buchstabensalat und schreib sie unter den richtigen Oberbegriff. Dann schreib fünf Sätze mit diesen Verben.*

paSsdoinghadstaygoingransitmakinggetupcamefinishedtellsayingSawtaking

| simple present | present progressive | simple past |
| --- | --- | --- |
| | | |
| | | |
| | | |
| | | |
| | | |

1.

2.

3.

4.

5.

*You are doing an interview with Morris, a great tennis star. Fill in the blanks with* many *or* much*, and then answer the questions for him.*

*Du führst ein Interview mit Morris, einem Tennisstar. Fülle die Lücken mit* many *oder* much *und beantworte die Fragen.*

How ___much___ do you practice every day?

I usually practice at least five hours a day, and sometimes more!

How ___________ money do you earn[1] by playing tennis?

______________________________________________

How ___________ tennis racquets[2] have you got?

______________________________________________

How ___________ tennis balls have you got?

______________________________________________

How ___________ fans have you got?

______________________________________________

How ___________ free time have you got before each match?

______________________________________________

How ___________ water do you drink before a match?

______________________________________________

How ___________ bananas do you eat after a match?

______________________________________________

How ___________ do you like playing tennis?

______________________________________________

[1] earn money = Geld verdienen
[2] tennis racquet = Tennisschläger

# Unit 6 – Überblick

## KV 6.1 What are you doing?

Diese Aufgabe übt gleichzeitig mehrere Grammatikformen. Die S müssen zuerst ein Personalpronomen mit der richtigen Form von *be* zusammensetzen, um damit das *present progressive* des Vollverbs zu bilden, und zuletzt die passenden Objekte auswählen.

## KV 6.2 Word partners

Diese KV präsentiert häufig verwendete Kollokationen. Aufgabe der S ist es, Verben mit passenden Phrasen zu verbinden. Eine mögliche Steigerung des Schwierigkeitsgrades wäre es, dass die S für ausgewählte Kollokationen zusammenhängende Sätze (in unterschiedlichen Zeitformen) aufschreiben.

## KV 6.3 I usually …

Diese Lückentextübung ermöglicht es den S, durch die vergleichende Gegenüberstellung ähnlicher Sätze im *simple present* und im *present progressive* den jeweiligen Bedeutungsunterschied zu festigen.

## KV 6.4 Jane's chores

Diese Schreibübung festigt das *present progressive*. Die S sollen zu jedem der Bilder zwei Sätze aufschreiben. Dabei sollen sie unter Verwendung des *present progressive* sagen, was Jane gerade macht, und eine Aussage darüber treffen, ob sie die entsprechende Tätigkeit auch mag.

## KV 6.5 *This/that* or *these/those*?

Diese Übung festigt den Unterschied zwischen *this/that* und *these/those*. Die S sollen das richtige Wort einsetzen, nachdem sie die Hinweise im Text *(here, over there, …)* erkannt haben.

## KV 6.6 Group words

Diese KV übt Wortschatz aus dem gesamten Band 1. Die S sollen für jede Lücke den passenden Oberbegriff der vorgegebenen Wörter einsetzen und ggf. noch weitere Beispiele aufschreiben.

## KV 6.7 You have to …

Diese Aufgabe übt Präpositionen rund um das Thema Party. Ein Kasten mit den Präpositionen ist als Hilfestellung vorhanden.

*Complete the sentences. Use the* present progressive.

*Vervollständige die Sätze. Benutze die Verlaufsform der Gegenwart.*

| | | | |
|---|---|---|---|
| I<br>You<br>He<br>She<br>Michael<br>Sarah<br>We<br>You<br>They | am<br>is<br>are | ~~eat~~<br>~~feed~~<br>go<br>listen<br>learn<br>look<br>play<br>read<br>talk<br>tidy<br>try on<br>wait<br>wash<br>watch<br>write | TV<br>the living room<br>a computer game<br>for the train<br>a newspaper<br>a poem<br>~~the cat~~<br>the dog<br>upstairs<br>at the board<br>~~a piece of cake~~<br>on the phone<br>to a CD<br>some English vocabulary<br>some jeans |

*I am eating a piece of cake.* ______________________________

*He is feeding the cat.* ______________________________

______________________________________________

______________________________________________

______________________________________________

______________________________________________

______________________________________________

______________________________________________

______________________________________________

______________________________________________

______________________________________________

______________________________________________

______________________________________________

______________________________________________

______________________________________________

**be** · up at six · happy · dressed · **do** · notes · a mess · **make**

to do the homework · yoga · dinner

piano

riding · a picnic · tired · shopping · swimming

ready (for) · sport · things ready

in a hurry

**play** · **go**

*All of the words and phrases can be matched to the verbs in the circles. Use different coloured pens to match the verb with its partners.*

*Alle Wörter und Phrasen können den eingekreisten Verben zugeordnet werden. Benutze verschiedene Farben für jedes Verb und ordne es seinen Partnern zu.*

photos · 10c off · out your books · a shower

breakfast · fun · your homework · home · guitar

off the train

to bed · on, tell me more!

football

**get** · models · on the bus · **take** · the exercises · **have**

*Complete the sentences. Use the words in the box.*

*Vervollständige die Sätze. Benutze die Wörter im Kasten.*

| What I/we usually/often/sometimes do (simple present) | What I/we are doing now/today (present progressive) |
|---|---|
| **1.** I usually wri*te*______ with a *pen*______. | **2.** Today I'm writ*ing*______ with a *pencil*______. |
| **3.** We usually pr______ new ______ together in class. | **4.** Now we ______ practic______ for our presentation together. |
| **5.** We sometimes r______ ______ books in the library. | **6.** Now we ______ read______ ______ books. |
| **7.** I usually si______ next to ______ in the classroom. | **8.** Today I ______ sit______ next to ______. |
| **9.** We often ______ in English lessons. | **10.** Now we ______ not talk______ because we ______ listen______ to a presentation. |
| **11.** I usually e______ a ______ in the morning break. | **12.** Today I ______ eat______ a ______ too. |
| **13.** I often l______ at the ______ in a lesson. | **14.** Now I ______ look______ at the ______. |
| **15.** I sometimes d______ ______ at lunch. | **16.** Today I ______ drink______ ______ at lunch. |
| **17.** We le______ a lot of English grammar every day. | **18.** Now we ______ learn______ about English tenses. |
| **19.** I sometimes st______ after class when I have got a ______. | **20.** Today I ______ not stay______ after class because it is Friday! |

sandwich • board • talk • John • teacher • banana • ~~pen~~ • question • vocabulary • Mary • ~~pencil~~ • English • German • milk • orange juice

*Jane likes weekends because she can do what she wants. But Jane's mother always gives Jane lots of things to do. Look at the pictures and write down what Jane is doing. Do you think she likes it? Use the* present progressive *and the* simple present.

*Jane mag Wochenenden, weil sie machen kann, was sie will. Aber Janes Mutter gibt ihr auch immer viele Aufgaben. Schau dir die Bilder an und beschreibe, was Jane gerade macht. Meinst du, sie mag, was sie tut? Benutze das* present progressive *und das* simple present.

**1.** *Jane's watching TV.*
*I think she likes it!*
____________________

**2.** *Jane's working in the garden.*
*I think she doesn't like it.*
____________________

**3.** ____________________
____________________
____________________

**4.** ____________________
____________________
____________________

5. ______________________________

______________________________

______________________________

6. ______________________________

______________________________

______________________________

7. ______________________________

______________________________

______________________________

8. ______________________________

______________________________

______________________________

# 6.5 KV *This/these or that/those?*

*Sarah and Pauline are shopping. Fill in the correct form of* this/these *or* that/those*.*

*Sarah und Pauline gehen einkaufen. Setz die richtige Form von* this/these *or* that/those *ein.*

**Remember:**

Wenn etwas näher beim Sprecher ist, verwendet man eher **this** und **these**.
Wenn etwas weiter entfernt ist, verwendet man eher **that** und **those**.

**Sarah** Look at ___these___ blue shoes in the corner of ___this___ window!
Do you like them? I think they look really cool.

**Pauline** Yes, but look over there in the second window, ____________ red flip flops are great!

**Sarah** Well, yes they are, but I need shoes for school. I can't wear flip flops to school!

**Pauline** Can you buy both ____________ blue shoes here for school and ____________ red flips flops for the summer holidays?

**Sarah** Maybe. Where is my money?

**Pauline** Oh, I've got it here in my bag. ____________ is your wallet[1], isn't it?

**Sarah** Yes, ____________'s my wallet. How much money have I got in it?

**Pauline** Hmm, you've got £ 20. Okay, let's go in and ask how much they are.

*(the girls go into the shop)*

**Sarah** Hello, I would like ____________ blue shoes in the corner of ____________ window over there. How much are they?

**Shop assistant** ____________ shoes are £ 32.

**Sarah** Oh, that's too expensive for me. But here are the flip flops again!
How much are ____________?

**Shop assistant** ____________ flip flops are £ 8.

**Sarah** Fantastic! I'll take them in a size 8.

**Pauline** Me too!

[1] wallet = Geldbeutel

*Fill in the group words in the chart. Can you think of more words?*

*Setz die Oberbegriffe in die Tabelle ein. Fallen dir weitere Wörter ein?*

| group words | vocabulary | more words |
| --- | --- | --- |
| *body* | eye, ear, leg | *head, foot* |
| *colours* | red, green | *blue, yellow* |
| ____________ | England | ____________ |
| ____________ | Monday, Tuesday | ____________ |
| ____________ | lemonade, milk | ____________ |
| ____________ | mother, brother | ____________ |
| ____________ | sandwich, potato | ____________ |
| ____________ | apple, orange | ____________ |
| ____________ | music, collecting stamps | ____________ |
| ____________ | hutch, cage | ____________ |
| ____________ | English, German | ____________ |
| ____________ | A, d, L, w | ____________ |
| ____________ | sausages, chicken | ____________ |
| ____________ | pound, cent | ____________ |
| ____________ | January, March | ____________ |
| ____________ | expensive ◀▶ cheap | ____________ |
| ____________ | dog, cat | ____________ |
| ____________ | he, it, we | ____________ |
| ____________ | kitchen, dining room | ____________ |
| ____________ | small, medium, XL | ____________ |
| ____________ | football, tennis, basketball | ____________ |
| ____________ | Maths, Geography, Science | ____________ |
| ____________ | cake, chocolate | ____________ |
| ____________ | 10 o'clock, half past two | ____________ |

# KV You have to ...

*Alex is having a party and his parents have a lot of instructions for him. Fill in the correct prepositions.*

*Alex veranstaltet eine Party und seine Eltern haben viele Anweisungen für ihn. Setz die richtigen Präpositionen ein.*

| | | |
|---|---|---|
| First, invite them | to | your party! |
| Tell them where they get | off | the bus, near our house. |
| Get everything ready | | your guests. You need lots of food! |
| When they come in, welcome your guests | | your home. |
| Have them come | | to the living room. |
| Find | | what they like to eat and drink. |
| Pass | | the food to all of your guests |
| Don't tell them "Hurry | | and finish eating!" |
| Wait | | all of your guests to come before you start eating the cake. |
| Ask your guests | | their hobbies. |
| Share your games | | your guests! They are your friends! |
| Don't worry | | the mess until after the party. |
| Always write thank you notes[1] | | your friends for the presents! |

about • around • for • in • off • out • to • up • with

[1] thank you letter = Dankesbrief

# Lösungen

## Unit 1

### 1.2 How we say and write dates

Janice's birthday is on 23$^{rd}$ July.
Janice's birthday is on the twenty-third of July.
Valentine's Day is on 14$^{th}$ February.
Valentine's Day is on the fourteenth of February.
Christmas is on 25$^{th}$ of December.
Christmas is on the twenty-fifth of December.

### 1.3 Dominos

exercises, exercise, shops, shop, dogs, dog, boxes, box, teachers, teacher, plates, plate, pencils, pencil, friends, friend, families, family, kites, kite, rulers, ruler, babies, baby, schools, school

### 1.4 Make your own sentences

1. The English teacher is nice.
2. I have got a new friend.
3. The teacher is at the new school.
4. We like English.
5. I am a new student at this school.
6. We have got a new friend.
7. I am ten years old.
8. This pupil is at an old school.
9. We can go to school.
10. This is an old English book.

### 1.5 Calendar word search

| | | | | | | | | | | | | | | |
|---|---|---|---|---|---|---|---|---|---|---|---|---|---|---|
| A | S | K | T | N | U | J | V | F | B | D | X | C | Z | D |
| O | B | M | J | A | N | U | A | R | Y | E | B | M | F | P |
| C | R | W | C | C | E | L | W | I | X | C | L | A | L | E |
| T | U | E | S | D | A | Y | Y | D | I | E | O | P | Y | O |
| O | Q | D | Z | X | F | Z | N | A | W | M | A | R | C | H |
| B | I | N | J | T | G | M | A | Y | H | B | K | I | D | N |
| E | P | E | L | H | Q | O | Y | W | V | E | T | L | X | F |
| R | H | S | E | P | T | E | M | B | E | R | V | Z | N | M |
| A | O | D | S | I | H | Y | O | Z | U | U | A | S | O | G |
| G | F | A | M | R | U | P | N | A | G | B | Q | C | V | R |
| B | N | Y | U | J | R | V | D | H | T | J | J | L | E | H |
| D | O | M | L | K | S | X | A | U | G | U | S | T | M | P |
| S | A | T | U | R | D | A | Y | L | S | N | J | D | B | I |
| C | E | P | N | Q | A | W | I | R | K | E | E | J | E | R |
| S | U | N | D | A | Y | Q | F | E | B | R | U | A | R | Y |

### 1.6 Colours cryptogram

| A | B | C | D | E | F | G | H | I | J | K | L | M |
|---|---|---|---|---|---|---|---|---|---|---|---|---|
| 18 | 14 | 16 | 2 | 12 | X | 3 | 21 | 22 | X | 26 | 6 | 10 |

| N | O | P | Q | R | S | T | U | V | W | X | Y | Z |
|---|---|---|---|---|---|---|---|---|---|---|---|---|
| 13 | 4 | 8 | X | 1 | 7 | 25 | 15 | X | 5 | X | 17 | X |

yellow + blue = green
white + red = pink
red + yellow = orange
pink + blue = purple
Question: How many colours are in a rainbow?
Answer: 7. Red, orange, yellow, green, blue, indigo, violet.

## Unit 2

### 2.1 Match the verbs

| | | |
|---|---|---|
| (sich) duschen | to have a shower | has a shower |
| lesen | to read | reads |
| putzen | to clean | cleans |
| machen | to do | does |
| schlafen | to sleep | sleeps |
| trinken | to drink | drinks |
| schreiben | to write | writes |
| stellen | to put | puts |
| füttern | to feed | feeds |
| (sich) streiten | to argue | argues |
| (sich) waschen | to wash | washes |
| tragen | to wear | wears |
| passen | to fit | fits |
| beobachten | to watch | watches |
| geben | to give | gives |
| essen | to eat | eats |
| kommen | to come | comes |
| erzählen | to tell | tells |

## 2.2 Michael's school day

Michael has breakfast at quarter to eight.
Michael takes the bus at half past eight.
He is at school at five minutes past nine.
He has lunch at twelve o'clock in the afternoon.
He comes home at quarter to four.
He does his homework at four o'clock.
He plays football at twenty past five.
He eats with his family at half past six.
He plays computer games at quarter past eight.
He goes to bed at ten past nine.

## 2.3 Family cryptogram

| A | B | C | D | E | F | G | H | I | J | K | L | M |
|---|---|---|---|---|---|---|---|---|---|---|---|---|
| 10 | 3 | 16 | 19 | 7 | X | 26 | 2 | 4 | X | X | 21 | 12 |

| N | O | P | Q | R | S | T | U | V | W | X | Y | Z |
|---|---|---|---|---|---|---|---|---|---|---|---|---|
| 1 | 20 | 11 | X | 24 | 13 | 5 | 14 | X | X | X | X | X |

parents' parents
grandparents' daughter
mother's brother
mother's sister
aunt and uncle's children
grandparents' grandchild
parents' children

## 2.4 Scrambled family words

father, grandchild, aunt, son, mother, grandpa, daughter, brother, grandma, uncle, parents, sister, cousin, child.
Question: What's your family name?

## 2.5 Maggie's family tree

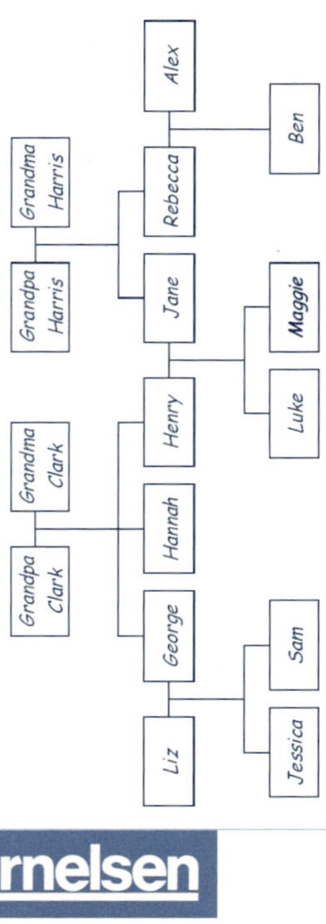


## 2.6 Pet shop ads

Pete, rabbit, carrots, water, sleeps, doesn't, has got. / Bobby, budgie, years old, sing, cage, blue, yellow. / Carlos, cat, milk, basket, black, white, needs.

## 2.7 Home sweet home

Lösung: There is no place like home!

# Unit 3

## 3.1 Sports Quiz

2 I do judo./I don't do judo.
3 I play tennis./I don't play tennis.
4 I go dancing./I don't go dancing.
5 I play badminton./I don't play badminton.
6 I go riding./I don't go riding.
7 I play American football./I don't play American football.

## 3.2 Laura's bedroom

| | | |
|---|---|---|
| 2 socks | 3 T-shirt | 4 boots |
| 5 shorts | 6 shirt | 7 jeans |
| 8 sweatshirt | 9 dress | 10 shoes |
| 11 football boots | | |

## 3.2 Where are Laura's clothes?

Her socks are on the bed. Her T-shirt is on the armchair. Her boots are in the wardrobe.
Her shorts are on the armchair. Her shirt is on the sofa. Her jeans are on the chair. Her sweatshirt is on the sofa. Her dress is in the wardrobe. Her shoes are under the desk.
Her football shoes are under the bed.

### 3.3 Opposites

boring ◄► interesting
first ◄► last
difficult ◄► easy
close ◄► open
new ◄► old
go to bed ◄► get up
big ◄► small
right ◄► wrong
full ◄► empty
good ◄► bad
question ◄► answer
before ◄► after
without ◄► with
out of ◄► into
goodbye ◄► hello
hate ◄► like
upstairs ◄► downstairs
night ◄► day
push ◄► pull
give ◄► take
always ◄► never

### 3.4 Shopping

1 **Shop Assistant:** Good morning. Can I help you?
2 **Mrs. Graham:** Yes, please. We need a new dress for my daughter. Size M, please.
3 **Amy:** Mum, do I have to wear a dress? I hate dresses.
4 **Mrs. Graham:** Yes, you have to wear a dress. I'm sorry Amy. You can't wear your jeans to your grandfather's 75th birthday party.
5 **Amy:** Well, OK. But can I have new jeans too?
6 **Mrs. Graham:** Maybe. Your favourite colours are red and blue, right? What about that dress?
7 **Amy:** No, I don't like red and blue, I like blue and green.
8 **Shop Assistant:** OK. Here you are, a size M blue and green dress.
9 **Mrs. Graham:** Thank you. Try it on, Amy.
10 **Shop Assistant:** Does it fit?
11 **Amy:** Yes, the dress fits.
12 **Shop Assistant:** Do you like it?
13 **Amy:** No, I don't like the dress, but I have to wear it anyway.
14 **Mrs. Graham:** Amy! We'll take it, and thank you very much for your help.
15 **Amy:** Sorry. Now can we look for jeans?

### 3.5 Pounds and pence, euros and cents

| | |
|---|---|
| seventy-nine cents | €0.79 |
| three pounds seventy-five p | £3.75 |
| one pound ninety-nine p | £1.99 |
| nine pounds sixty-five p | £9.65 |
| two-hundred thirty-three pounds fifty p | £233.50 |
| five euros ninety-six cents | €5.96 |
| fifty p | 50p |
| six pounds thirty-seven p | £6.37 |
| eighty-three p | 83p |
| thirty-four pounds twenty-one p | £34.21 |
| two euros eighty-seven cents | €2.87 |

### 3.6 Michael's week

3 Michael usually does homework.
4 Michael often plays football.
5 Michael usually lays the table.
6 Michael never plays the guitar.
7 Michael always feeds his rabbit.
8 Michael often plays hockey.
9 Michael never collects stamps.
10 Michael sometimes listens to a CD.

### 3.7 Maggie visits her grandparents

Where, Who, When, What, What, When, Who, Where

## Unit 4

### 4.1 Birthday invitation

| A | B | C | D | E | F | G | H | I | J | K | L | M |
|---|---|---|---|---|---|---|---|---|---|---|---|---|
| 11 | 19 | 10 | 5 | 22 | 15 | 25 | 13 | 18 | X | 20 | 14 | 3 |

| N | O | P | Q | R | S | T | U | V | W | X | Y | Z |
|---|---|---|---|---|---|---|---|---|---|---|---|---|
| 24 | 26 | 7 | X | 12 | 17 | 8 | 1 | 4 | 16 | X | 2 | X |

Dear Classmates,

I want to invite you to my birthday party. The party starts at three o'clock on Saturday afternoon. It is a fancy-dress party, so please wear funny clothes! I am making lots of food, mmm! See you then!

Sarah

### 4.2 At Sarah's party

are coming, are ringing, is opening, are saying, is taking, is putting, is inviting, is putting, is passing, is eating, is drinking, is opening, are leaving, 'm eating

### 4.3 A bottle of …

| | |
|---|---|
| 1 plate | 2 bowl |
| 3 bottle | 4 jug |
| 5 packet | 6 slices |
| 7 bottle, glass | 8 basket |

### 4.4 My body

**arm**: shoulder, hand, fingers.
**leg**: knee, foot/feet, toes.
**head**: hair, face, ear, eye, nose, mouth, tooth/teeth

### 4.5 *Some* or *any*?

2 any – Yes I need some pencils for school. /No, I don't need any pens for school.
3 any – Yes, I've got some photos of friends in my room. /No, I haven't got any photos of friends in my room.
4 some – Yes, I would like some new books. /No, I wouldn't like any new books.
5 any – Yes, I've got some computer games. /No, I haven't got any computer games.
6 any – Yes, there are some lamps in my room. /No, there aren't any lamps in my room.
7 any – Yes, I've got some food in my room. /No, I haven't got any food in my room.

### 4.6 Personal pronouns

| | |
|---|---|
| 3 it | 4 me |
| 5 it | 6 us |
| 7 him | 8 you |
| 9 them | 10 her |
| 11 you | 12 them |
| 13 her | 14 it |
| 15 him | 16 us |
| 17 it | 18 them |
| 19 you | 20 it |

### 4.7 Funny food

2 No, thank you. I'd like milk on my cornflakes.
3 No, thank you. I'd like marmalade on my toast.
4 No, thank you. I'd like apples /oranges /bananas in my fruit salad.
5 No, thank you. I'd like salad/ carrots /potatoes /a roll with my chicken.
6 No, thank you. I'd like milk and chocolate in my hot chocolate.
7 No, thank you. I'd like cheese and meat in my sandwich.

## Unit 5

### 5.1 Did you …?

3 They learned English, and Latin and French too.
4 They didn't listen to CDs or watch DVDs.
5 They only talked in class when the teacher said it was OK.
6 They played outside in the breaks.
7 The teachers helped them when they had a question.
8 They had P. E., but my mum didn't like running.
9 They didn't drink water in the classroom.
10 They used books in class.
11 They played after school in their free time.
12 My mum liked school, but she liked summer holidays best.

### 5.2 When I was your age …

walked, started, finished, had, had, didn't have, were, had, wasn't, shouted, didn't like, told, talked, didn't do, came, did, was, finished

### 5.3 What did Michael do yesterday?

Michael ran for the bus at quarter past eight.
He sat in class at five past nine.
He saw his friends at half past twelve.
He was back home twenty past three.
He did his homework at ten past four.
He played football at half past five.
He hurt his foot at five to six.
He made a model at ten to seven.
He watched TV at five past eight.
He went to bed at half past nine.

## 5.4 Match the verbs

be → was/were
come → came
do → did
get up → got up
go → went
have → had
laugh → laughed
make → made
run → ran
say → said
see → saw
sit → sat
tell → told
take → took
talk → talked

## 5.5 Tangrams

1.

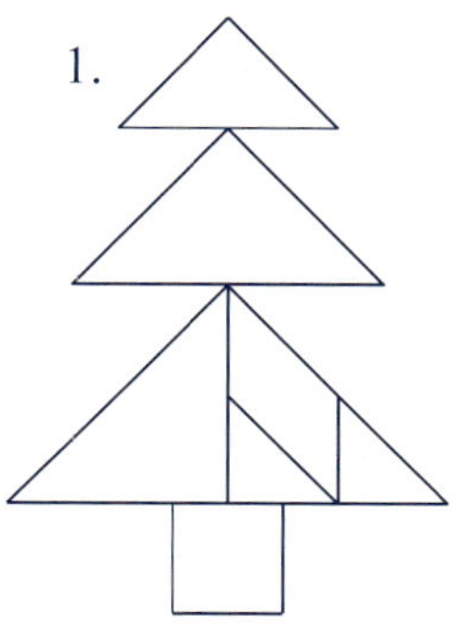

2.

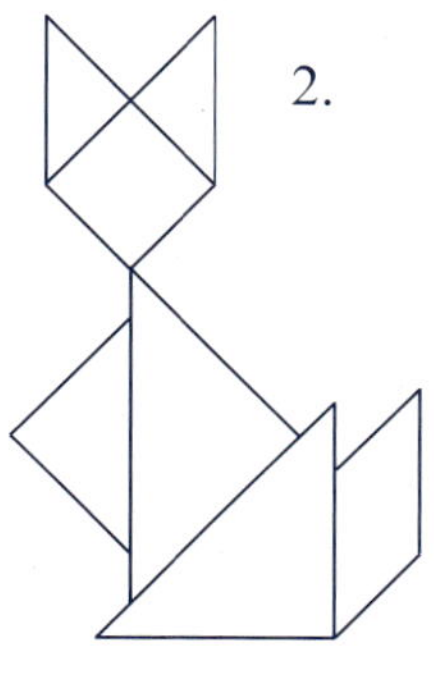

3.

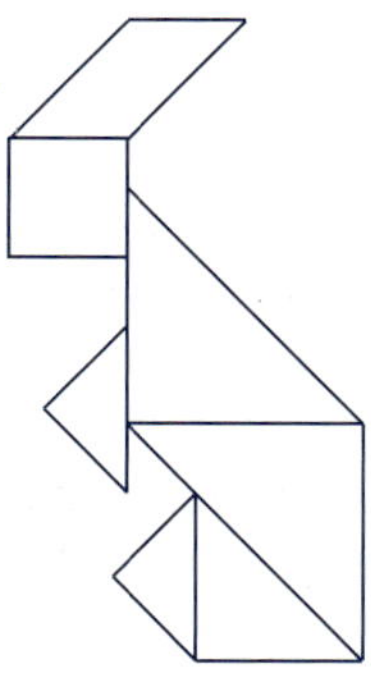

4.

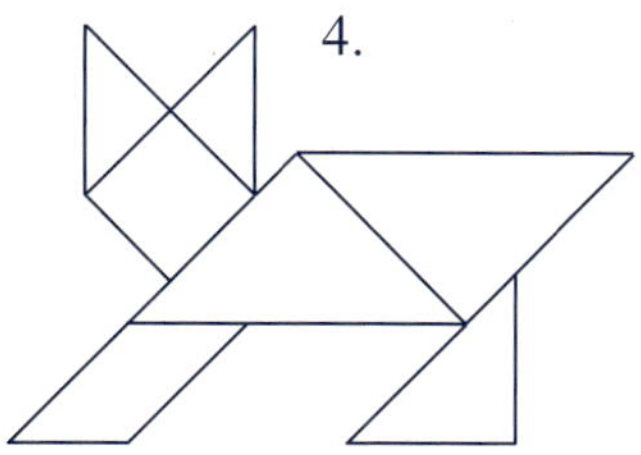

5.

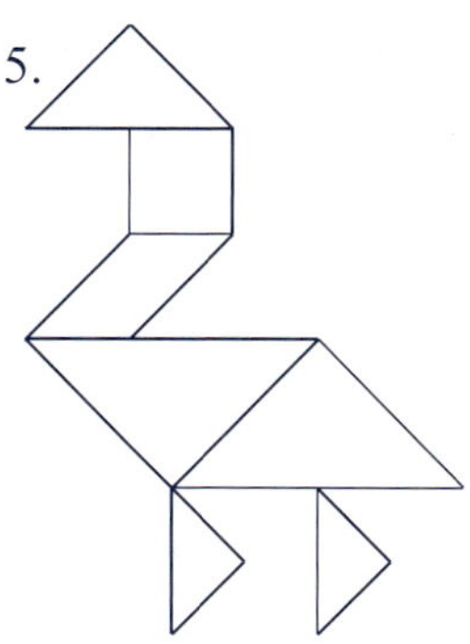

## 5.6 Letter mix

**simple present:** pass, get up, stay, sit , tell
**present progressive:** doing , going, making, taking, saying
**simple past:** came, finished, had, ran, saw

## 5.7 Morris the tennis star

much – I earn lots of money by playing tennis.
many – I have got five tennis racquets.
many – I have got thirty tennis balls.
many – I have got at least a hundred fans!
much – I usually have got an hour of free time before each match.
much – I drink lots of water before a match.
many – I never eat bananas after a match. I don't like bananas!
much – I like playing tennis a lot!

# Unit 6

## 6.1 What are you doing?

going → upstairs
listening → to a CD
learning → some English vocabulary
looking → at the board
playing → a computer game
reading → a newspaper
talking → on the phone
tidying → the living room
trying on → some jeans
waiting → for the train
washing → the dog
watching → TV
writing → a poem

## 6.2 Word partners

**take:** out your books, 10c off, notes, photos
**have:** a picnic, a shower, breakfast, dinner, fun, to do the homework
**do:** your homework, sport, yoga, the exercises
**make:** a mess, models
**get:** up at six, ready for, things ready, dressed, off the train, get on the bus
**be:** happy, tired, in a hurry
**go:** home, on, tell me more!, riding, shopping, swimming, to bed
**play:** football, guitar, piano

### 6.3 I usually …

3 practice, vocabulary
4 are, practicing
5 read, English/German
6 are, reading, German/English
7 sit, John/Mary
8 am, sitting, Mary/John
9 talk
10 are, talking, are, listening
11 eat, banana/sandwich
12 am, eating, sandwich/banana
13 look, board/teacher
14 am, looking, teacher/board
15 drink, orange juice/milk
16 am, drinking, milk/orange juice
17 learn
18 are, learning
19 stay, question
20 am, staying

### 6.4 Jane's chores

3 Jane's cleaning her room. I think she doesn't like it.
4 Jane's playing soccer with a friend. I think she likes it.
5 Jane's practicing the piano. I think she doesn't like it.
6 Jane's reading a book. I think she likes it.
7 Jane's doing her homework. I think she doesn't like it.
8 Jane's playing a computer game. I think she likes it.

### 6.5 *This/these* or *that/those*?

those, these, those, This, that, those, that, Those, these, Those

### 6.6 Group words

countries – Germany
days of the week – Wednesday
drinks – orange juice
family – sister
food – bread
fruit – banana
hobbies – playing computer games
homes for pets – basket
languages – French
letters – e
meat – hamburger
money – euro
months – February
opposites – big ◂▸ small
pets – budgie
pronouns – she
rooms – bedroom
sizes – L
sports – hockey
subjects – English
sweets – ice cream
times – 3 o'clock

### 6.7 You have to …

for, to, in, out, round, up, for, about, with, about, to